Sally Mundell

PACKAGING
GOOD

The Healing Therapy of Giving

Sally Mundell

authorHOUSE®

AuthorHouse™
1663 Liberty Drive
Bloomington, IN 47403
www.authorhouse.com
Phone: 1 (800) 839-8640

Published by AuthorHouse 11/08/2017

ISBN: 978-1-5462-1513-4 (sc)
ISBN: 978-1-5462-1512-7 (e)
ISBN: 978-1-5462-1511-0 (hc)

Library of Congress Control Number: 2017916795

Contents

Preface ix

Part 1: Suddenly: My Story of Love and Loss 1

Part 2: In the Twinkling: Our Time to Grieve 20

Part 3: This Special Place: The Packaged Good Story 28

Part 4: Carry On: Ten Lessons Learned to Grow through Pain 47

Part 5: My Happy Place: A Guide to Giving Back 63

Appendix: A Collection of Poems by Grover Mundell 81

References 95

Message of Gratitude 97

In honor of and inspired by
Grover Mundell
1964–2013

Preface

My parents called me Pistol-Packing Momma. I was a sassy five-year-old, and I *lived* in my favorite red and white sequin cowgirl tap dance costume. The white tassels hung from my legs, while my white Stetson sat tilted on top of my red curls. My holsters held two black pistols, ready for action. During my dance recital, the other girls and I worked the stage. My hair bounced and my pug nose wrinkled, as I tapped furiously. As family lore has it, although I don't remember, at the end of the performance, I silenced the crowd by yelling, "Pistol-Packing Momma," as I placed my guns back in the holster. I was tough, tenacious, fearless, and those traits would suit me well down the road. But little did I know that thirty years later, I would be filled with fear and find myself in need of much more than a stiff upper lip to overcome tragedy, after losing my husband and the father of my two daughters. I would come to learn the power of vulnerability and discover the gift of channeling grief into giving to truly heal the heart. It would be the most valuable lesson I've ever learned and one that I am motivated to share with my girls and with you readers.

Part 1

Suddenly: My Story of Love and Loss

Suddenly

If I could make you pause and appreciate the wondrous stars that shine at night along with the moon and the planets twinkling above,

If I could wrap up the raging rivers and the purple mountains and the lonely canyons deep with breathtaking vistas of lakes and trees and the wonderfully heartbreaking desolation of the desert, along with the simplicity of the taste of cool water and the indescribable smell of wild flowers and prairie grass after a spring rain, with all the beauty of creation wrapped together in a gift,

If I could take everything that has ever made you smile—every pleasure and every comfort—all your aspirations—all the dreams—everything that you have ever wanted to become or share or create—and make them all suddenly easily within your grasp,

If I could take it all and compress it into a single emotion—into the essence of love—and if I could give it to you each and every moment for the rest of my life,

Then I will call my life complete.

And suddenly,

I will say that we're even.

Because you—my dear—have already given all of these things to me.

Grover Mundell

For more poems, see the appendix.

1

It was the worst day of my life. I slowly walked, hair disheveled, eyes red, clothes wrinkled, pale and exhausted, down the long hospital hallway to the ICU, holding my two- and five-year-old daughters' hands. They were quiet and scared. I was quiet and scared. I was in a bad dream as I led them into a room filled with beeping machines, flashing red lights, and their father. At thirty-five years old, after seven years of marriage, I was saying goodbye to my love. Two months earlier, my husband, Grover, and I had been planning our goals for our future—a home renovation and amazing vacations—and then suddenly, there was no future. And prior goals became trivial. As I watched the girls tentatively approach their father in the hospital bed—his eyes closed, his face swollen, IVs and machines hooked into his bruised arms and his mouth—memories flashed by.

I was twenty-six years old, working in sales and marketing for a technology start-up in the legal industry, living in New York City, enjoying the single life—and I didn't see him coming.

"You were the highlight of my trip," he said to me.

I did a double-take. I had noticed this engaging fellow with gray hair and glasses in a suit throughout the weekend of legal conferences, meetings, and social gatherings in New York. Although he wore a tie, he seemed very approachable and easy-going. He taught a few classes that weekend at the conference, and rather than being bored with the content, the crowd was engaged and interacted with jokes and laughs. I was engaged. He made a rather dull topic about court reporting very entertaining. I was attracted to his energy, and I was curious about him and why he found me so interesting.

We had an instant spark, but he lived far away in Denver. As part of our courtship, he emailed me songs he'd sung and recorded for me: "And It Stoned Me" by Van Morrison, "Wonderful Tonight" by Eric Clapton (except he had changed the hair color to red for mine), and "Behind Blue Eyes" by the Who. His voice sounded great—it was strong, with a sensitive rasp that reminded me of Van himself, but maybe I was biased. I was in awe of him and had never met anyone who was so open, had so many talents, and possessed a curiosity to learn more and experience life in a way I hadn't. He was thirteen years my senior (a first time for me to date a much older man), but all of his experiences and wisdom added to the attraction.

I remember walking down the busy streets of Gramercy Park in New York with Grover's music pulsing on my iPod, sun shining in my face, smiling at the world. I was blinded by the overflowing feeling of love—so blinded that only the blaring horn and obscenities from a taxi driver could awake me from my daze. Yep, classic New York moment.

Because we both traveled for work and lived in different cities, we decided to date all over the United States. Our next dates were in Chicago, Orlando, Phoenix, Denver, and New York again. We got along like old friends and enjoyed every moment together. One date weekend in Chicago, we went to the John Hancock Observatory, at the time the tallest building in Chicago. They had a photographer to commemorate the moment. Neither one of us was very photogenic, but for some reason, we kept asking the guy over and over to take our picture, until he had taken more than ten of us. Afterward, we couldn't stop laughing because we looked so bad in the photographs. Being a naturally serious and intense person, I loved that he made me laugh a lot and enjoy the moment. He helped me to relax.

One of my favorite trips was visiting the wine country in Grand Junction, Colorado, which is a quaint town with beautiful scenery and romantic vineyards. It was New Year's Eve 2006, and we stayed at a bed and breakfast at the top of a hill that overlooked the town. That's when Grover proposed, overlooking the beautiful mountains of Grand Junction.

Six months later, on the night of our rehearsal dinner at an Italian restaurant on the main street of Grand Junction, I fell in love with Grover even more as I watched him read a poem called *Suddenly* (yes, the one at the beginning of this section) in front of all our friends and family.

My head stayed pretty much in the clouds as we began a life together, but we certainly had the normal ups and downs. In the first year of marriage, we moved three times between two different cities. We sold two condos. I had some issues with our first pregnancy and ended up having a miscarriage, which was really tough for both of us (see poem in appendix).

Over time, we recovered and tried again. This time, our perfect little Ruby was born. Northside Hospital, known in Georgia as the mecca for childbirth, was busy. A nurse who looked to be about fifteen years old was taking care of me. As the baby came out and I was screaming in pain and throwing towels across the room, she told Grover to grab a leg because the doctor was busy with someone else.

Grover stepped up and said, "No problem. I've delivered a lot of baby calves on the ranch where I grew up."

I don't think I appreciated being the cow, but maybe I found it funny. I can't remember. I saw Grover's eyes get big as the baby came out, and thankfully the doctor walked in right in time to catch Ruby.

Ruby was a feisty little girl and came out kicking and screaming. The nurse, who probably had delivered a thousand babies, even said, "You have a feisty one."

And we continued to see that spirit as Ruby got older. She has been fearless with rock climbing, zip lining, and diving into mud, and she is also a strong, independent girl who can't be told what to like and what to do. She will choose which sports to play, what clothes to wear, and it's even a negotiation on the going rate for chores. She will make sure her opinion is heard.

And then, two and a half years after Ruby was born, sweet Matilda was born. The cord was wrapped around her neck, and while our amazing doctor quickly unwrapped it, Grover and I waited anxiously for some noise. Matilda came out and remained quiet for what seemed an eternity. As a parent, you wait to hear for the scream after birth. You are supposed to hear a scream. Finally, I heard it and took a big breath. I'm not sure I was really worried, though, because I didn't feel that tragedy could happen to me.

Matilda started out my quiet, reserved child and grew into her strength over time. She was the one to sit on my lap and be a little more tentative about meeting new people. Today, she's still shy about making new friends, but her independence and strength are now on par with Ruby's, which makes them quite a pair with extreme sports and obstacle courses (as well as trying to parent). I am very fortunate to be raising strong, independent, fearless girls.

As with all parents, during the younger years, our weekends were a blur of parks and birthday parties. I look back on that period and remember being in survival mode. On top of raising the kids, we went through a home renovation, which was followed by an unfortunate rat infestation in our basement. We lived near a lake in the woods, and somehow a few rats found their way in and reproduced. It was horrible. We had two young kids and rats pretty much everywhere. One rat found a home behind our refrigerator. I had two little kids, and by God, I was going to get that sucker before it harmed a baby. I set up traps everywhere and ended up catching it myself. I paraded around in celebration. I had defended my family. That rat should have known better than to try to escape Pistol-Packing Momma.

In 2008, I joined Spanx, founded by Sara Blakely, the creator of the shapewear industry and the number one shapewear company in the United States. I rose in the ranks, and by the time I had the two girls, I was running the e-commerce business worldwide, overseeing a large team and a significant portion of the company's revenue. While life was crazy at times, I had a lot of pride in my job and what I was doing. I loved growing the team and the business and figuring out what was next and deciding how to optimize the business so it was more productive. Sara was inspirational, and the people who worked at Spanx were another family for me. I loved being with them and working with such a passionate and capable team. It was an exciting and special experience; I learned a ton and grew even more.

I had two beautiful children, a great husband, and a fantastic career. Things weren't always perfect, but the ship was heading in the right direction, and I felt fulfilled (if maybe overwhelmed and crazy at times). But in the winter of 2012, our ship started taking on some water. Grover and I got some type of flu-like respiratory illness. Lots of coughing, coupled with exhaustion; we couldn't shake it. We blamed it on having young kids. After about week three, we both started feeling better and began to get back to our normal routine. Small crisis seemingly averted.

2013 kicked into gear, and Grover seemed to relapse. He still wasn't feeling himself. He was tired, and I was busy and distracted with work and kids. I sort of resented him needing so much time to recover and largely leaving me to take care of the kids.

Grover's health continued to decline, and he began missing important events and work. He was now coughing up cups of mucus daily, although he was mostly doing it at work, so I didn't know the extent of it. I didn't understand how he could be so sick while getting plenty of medicine from the doctor. It's how I imagine many victims of natural disaster feel: something they had never seen before comes for their life, and they can't even fathom it. Grover was dying, but we had no idea.

Then on February 7, he just couldn't get out of bed. During the morning hustle with the kids, he called me to come help him; I walked into the room, and he was still in bed. I needed to call in some help. Raising a family requires a village. As I was juggling the kids by myself and had a work meeting with out of town attendees, I asked my brother Stan, an amazing human and always willing to help, if he could take Grover to the doctor. We thought he might have a particularly tough pneumonia, which was about the worst case we could imagine. This time, the doctor heard a crackling in his lungs, which we would later find out was the sign of a terrible lung disease.

The doctor had Stan take Grover directly to the hospital, so he could get the appropriate diagnosis and treatment. He stayed for the next month and never left. The first week was a parade of doctors ruling out over fifty different diseases while attempting to figure out what Grover had. We literally had a list of diseases and were crossing them out. Yay, no HIV.

Yay, no tuberculosis. But what is it? He was in a regular hospital bed, could talk normally and have conversations, but could not breathe normally and needed to rest all the time.

The next week, the doctors came to us and said they had narrowed it down to two different diseases, neither of which was promising. To know for sure, they had to do a biopsy, which is an antiseptic word for opening Grover up and cutting out a large portion of lung. It was all so scary and unreal, and happening so fast.

My parents and family continued to watch the girls while I spent the day at the hospital with Grover, being his advocate and caretaker. It was stressful recording all his medicines and making sure we followed all the doctors' instructions. There were so many doctors and nurses involved, so many procedures. Each day, I had to relay the medications and what had happened negatively or positively the previous day to the next group of doctors and nurses. I felt like I had his life in my hands. I had to make sure they gave the right medicine. I had to tell the new doctor his history over and over again. There were infectious disease doctors, pulmonary doctors, internal medicine doctors, the general case manager doctor, and all the nurses, and they changed every few days. I probably talked to over forty doctors and sixty nurses during the month we were at the hospital. But none of them could give us an answer. None of them could tell us our future. None of them could offer comfort for our worst fears.

> One doctor explained it this way: "When we hear hoof beats, we think horses, but when you came over the hill, it was more like a zebra, and we don't get many zebras coming through. On top of that, we needed to figure out what kind of zebra we were dealing with."

> Treatment should begin quickly for very ill patients, and everyone did exactly the right things in my case. It has been a marvel, however; I was getting worse and fast. I was gulping O_2 and requiring more and more. They wanted to conduct thoracic surgery now! Take lung samples sufficient

for pathologies that could explain what was happening, and they needed to do it ASAP. In the middle of all this, my brother and my moral compass—my mother—had aired up the tires on the truck, gotten tickets, and flown to my bedside. I looked at them and said, "Saddle up."

A very petite thoracic surgeon appeared and held up her hands; smiling down at me, she said, "Small hands, small holes."

Grover's journal, February 2013

The doctor came into Grover's small hospital room. There was only one chair for him to sit in, and I sat on Grover's bed. I could sense his nervous energy. In such a small room, it was intense. He sat down and began a prepared speech. The biopsy had come back with the worst-case scenario. I remember the doctor being so ambiguous about the impact of it all. I needed to know if Grover was dying: needed and dreaded. Then he said, "It sucks," and stopped talking. That's when I knew it was terminal, because who wants to tell a man and his wife who have two small children that there is very little hope? I now know "focus on quality of life" means your life is about to suck.

Grover had idiopathic pulmonary fibrosis (IPF), a disease of unknown origin that hardens the lungs to the point of suffocation. The advice from his team of doctors was to focus on quality of life. I got out my computer and researched. I read that the diagnosis comes with only two to three years left of life. However, the accelerated version most likely ends in death within four to six weeks.

"Did Grover have the accelerated version?" I asked the doctor, who didn't really give me a response. If he had the regular version, the only way to continue living is with oxygen tanks and a lung transplant.

Knowing death was peering over our shoulders, we spent the day talking and reconnecting. We cried, and we daydreamed about what a second chance at life would look like. It was just the two of us in the room, alone for hours, it felt like. Knowing what he had in some ways released the anxiety of not knowing. We knew what we were dealing with, so we could pause and figure out how to respond to it. Life stood still that day. We held hands, we cuddled. We *loved* each other.

"I'm going to take more vacations, start a foundation to help others get lung transplants, and spend more time with the girls," Grover told me. "My new life will be fantastic. I'm lucky I get a second chance to do it all right."

"And what happens if you don't make it?" I whispered sadly. "What am I supposed to do with the girls? What sort of life do you want me to carry on?"

He looked at me and said, "I can't tell you. I don't know what life will be like in five or ten years. I don't want to limit you with a dying wish."

"I'm so sorry I didn't realize how sick you were," I said, not wanting any regrets. "I'm so sorry I wasn't paying more attention. Please forgive me."

He smiled and said, "I love you. We are going to get through this, and one day I'll write about it."

Any walls we had built up over the years were now down. We were both being so raw with each other, it was a higher level of love than we had ever experienced. The illness had given us a deeper level of intimacy. We were present, we were alive, we were in love. I would have never imagined feeling so connected, so loved in this situation. A gift out of the tragedy.

And Grover was just amazing with his attitude. He owned quality of life. His attitude was in his control. There was a sign on the wall that said, "What is your pain scale?" with an option of 1-10. He took the sign and crossed out "pain" and replaced it with "joy," so it read "What is your joy scale?" Even a dying man can choose to be happy. I learned so much from him those days in the hospital.

> Positive Energy is on my mind. And I owe it all to Interstitial (Idiomonary) Pulmonary Fibrosis and to so many friends and family. IPF is a degenerative disease.

Basically, fibrosis means hardening, interstitial refers to the part of the cellular walls that become necrotic with this condition. There is no spontaneous recovery with this. There is no clinical treatment for this. Some people decline more slowly, others more quickly, and others stair-step down; I think this is mainly dependent on what kind of zebra you are dealing with and what kind of lion you carry inside of you. Life expectancy is 3 to 5 years. I am in a fantastic position to vastly improve these statistics by getting lung transplantation at the appropriate moment and snatching victory from the jaws of defeat. I might be overly confident frankly, but this is where the positive energy comes into play. I have not only the best possible medical team assembled and 100% engaged on my case already, but I have weapons the likes of which cannot not be adequately described with English language. I have all of you!

I get the question "what can we do to help" and I am willing to work with you and welcome the opportunity to make positive things happen not just for myself but for my family and for you and for as many as possible. The answer is to be positive and to generate positive energy and send it to me. I will bounce it back to you 2 fold. This will make even more people smile and together we will change the world for the better. I commented to Sally yesterday what a great day I had that we spent together. A day that I would not trade for 100s of others. Please do not gather horned toads and sacrifice them on hot rocks on my behalf. My family are a musical sort and I am as well. So make music, dance, sing, laugh and let those good vibrations ring out to me. Raise your glass and send me a toast. I have always preferred a celebration to a commiseration and a feast to a fast. I believe in health through positive energy. We decide the polarization of our own battery in our hearts and minds and the universe complies with our decisions. Growing up in Baca County there were times that I went looking for a fight and every single time I found one. And I regretted every single one of them. I am not in a fight against disease. I am too consumed with joy and gratitude for fighting. Maybe I quibble too much with semantics and you might think these words are weak but you would be gravely mistaken to think so. What I am struggling to say is simply to be happy, fill up on positive vibes and pass them to me, help me fill myself with gratitude and joy leaving no room for anything else.

Grover's Facebook Message, February 2013

The doctors said for Grover to get placed on the lung transplant list, his body had to be in decent shape. We worked to get him there. He had been laying in the hospital for almost three weeks now. We practiced walking down the hallway and breathing into these tools that looked like inhalers that helped strengthen the lungs. He had to blow a ball up the chamber. We tried to stay positive, as it hardly moved. And we began praying. Grover willed us all to have hope.

Through all of Grover's illness, I was still working at Spanx. While they were great and allowed me to be at his side the whole time, I still was responsible for a large portion of business. My days would consist of checking emails for an hour or two, taking care of Grover at the hospital for five or six hours, and then going home to take care of the girls. I was exhausted. This went on for four weeks. Grover needed a lot of help, so I waited on him for anything I could do to ease discomfort or pain. I remember trying to finish an email while he was asking for help reaching something.

I yelled, "Give me a minute. I'm trying to do it all, but I can't."

He responded, "I'm just trying to live. I am just trying to breathe over here." He said it with humor, but I could tell it pained him to be so helpless.

I ran out of the room, down the hallway, and just cried. I couldn't handle it anymore. I wanted work to distract me, anything to distract me from what was happening. I tucked into a corner in the hospital corridor and bawled. A nurse stopped by and asked if I was okay. I said yes, but of course I wasn't. I was breaking.

My parents brought Ruby and Matilda each to a bed-and-breakfast near the hospital, and I spent one night with each of them, so I could give them my full attention. Matilda, at two years old, showed up in a princess dress and her purple cast on her broken arm from jumping off the couch a few weeks prior. It made me smile to see her. We played with toys and cuddled together in the bed. It was so good to be with my girls. I wanted to tell them it was going to be okay, but I just didn't know. When it was Ruby's turn, at age five, she had a lot more thoughts running through her head. She seemed to be thinking something in her head and was not sure of our situation.

After a few minutes of exploring the B&B and playing, she looked at me and said, "Are you giving us away?"

I burst into tears. I was so focused on taking care of Grover, I hadn't fully explained to them what was going on (nor did I know what to say). All the girls knew is that they had been shuffled around for a month among my family, and that their daddy was sick. It broke my heart. I hadn't read the manual for this chapter of parenting; I had not been trained to tell my kids that their daddy could die.

As I write this book four years later, Ruby, now nine years old, says to me, "I thought Daddy was just sick like he had to get a tooth out at the doctor. I didn't understand. I thought you were giving me away."

Kids live in these traumatic moments as if they were yesterday, and we must work through them many years later.

My sister-in-law took Matilda to get the cast removed while I was preoccupied in the hospital. Two years after it happened, Matilda asked me, "Where were you? I needed my mommy. I was scared when they took off the cast."

I will never know what losing their daddy or that time period did to my girls, but we are no longer afraid to face those feelings anytime they arise.

Grover continued to stay positive, as I slowly fell apart.

> Oh baby don't worry. We are so blessed. I'm afraid to go to sleep and wake up tubed because I dipped below 85 oxygen level. I will take the first watch. You rest easy honey. Know that I love you. We're so close now I can see paradise and its right here with you my love.
>
> There is nothing in this world but you for me. For now and forever. I thought that nothing could possibly change that in any way when we married. Then we created a family and it did change, it got even better and if life gets any better I will lose my mind.
>
> Text Message from Grover, Feb 2013

Some days, it was hard to believe Grover was really that sick. I remember us being in the ICU: me, Grover, his brother, and his mother. There was nowhere to sit, so his mom sat on the toilet that was just out in the open. Always being a jokester, Grover thought it was funny and took a picture of his mom and shared it on Facebook. We laughed. That was two weeks before he died.

"Sally, promise me you'll start a foundation," Grover said one day while he pulled the oxygen mask away from his face. "We need to do more. We need to give back. I realize it now. Don't wait until I'm better. Please do it now. Help me get a set of lungs."

His sense of urgency came from realizing there weren't enough lungs to go around. Not enough people sign up to be organ donors, so people die on the waiting list for lungs. And his chances were slim. He laid out the foundation plans on pieces of paper and gave them to me.

He also had me keep notes about what all was happening to him, so he could write a book of how he overcame the disease one day. He would randomly tell me things to record throughout the day as they popped into his head: "There needs to be a manual for how to breath into the CPAP machine … it's important for one to express gratitude no matter what shape they are in to improve the quality of life." I jotted the notes down as he spouted out his random thoughts throughout the day.

Grover continued to push me to start calling around to see what we could do to start helping other people while we spent our days waiting for doctors, so when Sara Blakely, founder of Spanx, reached out to me to ask me how she could help, I told her that Grover's focus was on helping other people the last days of his life. Amazingly, Sara, a huge philanthropist, knew just what to do and donated money on Grover's behalf to the Pulmonary Fibrosis Foundation. I couldn't believe how amazing and generous she was.

Grover smiled when I told him and said, "See, we can start making a difference. This is just beginning."

But his smile was mixed with sadness. He was in more pain and was getting more scared every moment. I am so appreciative of what Sara did for me and my family during that whole period. That moment created an amazing memory for us and provided Grover relief that he was making a difference.

While Grover stayed optimistic, his health continued to decline. The doctors wanted to transfer him to Emory Hospital, where there was a specialist in his disease and a transplant team. We just had to wait for a bed to open up. It was crazy, but we had to wait for someone to get better or die for him to transfer. Finally, we got the call. We celebrated and braced ourselves for the move. Grover would go by ambulance. He was very sick and would need a massive amount of oxygen; they had to gently lift him onto a gurney. His breathing had gotten so bad that he had to remain still to keep his breathing consistent.

While we waited for the ambulance, Grover started getting antsy after weeks upon weeks laying in the hospital bed. He also had a massive amount of steroids shooting through his veins, as well as an increase in anxiety around moving him to the new hospital. He started checking emails and texts and was trying to text "Happy Birthday" on Facebook to someone. I asked him to please stop checking his phone and relax and focus on breathing. He needed all his energy for the move.

He got really angry and yelled, "I just want to send a happy birthday message."

The yell set off his lungs and took all his air, and he started spiraling down. The machine started blinking red and beeping. His body convulsed trying to get air in its lungs, and his eyes rolled back. The nurses ran in. Our argument was killing him. He wasn't ready to die. He was trying so hard to stay positive, to the point of denial. All I could think was, *I've just killed him. This is the moment.* There was a good minute where I thought that it was over, but he pulled himself back and was able to control his breathing. Slowly, his oxygen level rose, and his eyes adjusted. These episodes had been flaring up more frequently, but this was by far the worst. He wasn't going to come back next time. We both realized it, and we were scared. It was critical to make it to Emory. It was our only chance (see poem "Make it on to Emory" in appendix).

Grover had a lot of visitors to the hospital over the month: friends, his family from Colorado, and my family. We constantly had people visiting, but at the worst moments, we were alone. It's hard to have people around when you are going through something so difficult. It's stressful, and there's really nothing others can do to help inside a small hospital room.

Thankfully, the ambulance drivers loaded him into their vehicle, and he made it all the way to the hospital without an episode. I drove by myself, alone and scared behind the ambulance. I slept the night in a visitor chair that reclines into a bed right outside his room. He would text me to come in and see him throughout the night. He was scared. His optimism was gone, and realization had set in.

In the morning, the doctor came to me and asked to speak privately. He showed me Grover's chest x-rays and said, "There is really nothing we can do for him."

His lungs had almost completely shut down. The x-rays of the lungs showed two lungs all filled in with white. I walked back into the room, crying and trying to figure out how I tell my husband he was going to die. Grover knew. He was surrounded by nurses and doctors and machines, and everything was loud, but the moment I came in, it all got silent.

I told him, "He said it doesn't look good."

Through the oxygen mask, Grover said, "We knew it would come to this." It was like watching a movie, but I was in it. It couldn't be real. It did indeed suck. And those were his last words.

Then Grover's lungs gave up on him. Machines started to go off. The doctors asked me to leave, so they could sedate and intubate him.

I thought, *So that's it*, and I cried and cried, comforted by my family.

Later that day, the transplant team reached out to me and told me they had gotten him on the transplant list! It was a small miracle! They told me that they would work harder than ever since Grover had such young kids and wife. He and we deserved a second chance. Most people who have this illness are in their seventies or eighties. I think they had even more empathy for us being so young. Grover was forty-eight, and I was thirty-five years old with a two- and five-year-old. I was so excited. I celebrated with my family and friends. I knew it would be a hard road, but it meant life and a second chance. We were going to make it!

Grover was intubated and then sedated. They attempted waking him up a few times, since they would need to be able to wake him up, remove the tubes, and have him stable to do a lung transplant. The doctors asked me to come for one of the times to help keep him calm. It's really scary to have all this equipment inside your body, replacing the function of your organs. Grover kept panicking when they would wake him up.

He woke up for a minute, and I told him, "It's going to be okay. The girls love you. You are going to get a transplant."

He gave me two thumbs up, as much as he could with all the IVs and machines hooked up to him. He looked bewildered and scared and no longer like the optimistic Grover I knew. I hope my words comforted him. They put him back to sleep.

Unfortunately, our excitement was short-lived, and the next day, they had to take Grover off the transplant list. His body was too sick, and the transplant team, being overly optimistic, had fed us false hope. The likelihood he would have survived the transplant in his condition was less than a percentage point, and they didn't want to "waste" a good pair of lungs. I often wonder if it would have been better had they just told me there was no hope. Who knows? We did have hope until the very end. And then it became the end.

After a month-long roller coaster of emotion, fighting for Grover's life, the doctor told me the words every spouse in the hospital dreads: "There is nothing more we can do for him."

It was time for me to go get the girls. I had spoken to the children's therapist, who said the girls needed to say good-bye to him. They needed closure and to know what really happened, no matter how painful it was. I knew it was the right call. I'd want that for myself, and I needed to give that opportunity to the girls. They had only seen him a few times in the hospital, and I'm not sure they fully understood what was going on.

Crying, I drove home alone to get my girls, giving myself a pep talk to hold it together for them. I needed to now take the role as caregiver and supporter and let my girls grieve. I opened the door to see two little girls laughing and playing. They were singing and dancing around in princess outfits. Stuffed animals were lined up surrounding them on the floor. I had to take a moment to adjust to the happy environment. It felt as if I'd entered another world. They saw me and ran to me excitedly.

I kneeled and said, "Girls, I need to talk to you." They tentatively and curiously came to me, as my tone became serious. I looked my daughters in the eyes and said, "We need to go say good-bye to your daddy. He's dying." I kept it short; otherwise, the words would not have come out, only tears.

Of course, they had no concept really what that meant, but they could tell by my tone it was serious. The nanny, who had been with us for four years, heard me and let out a wail. I gave her a hug. I hugged the girls and silently got them into the car. I drove to the hospital silently, with tears streaming down my face, trying to pull myself together for what would be the hardest thing I hope I'll ever have to do as a mother.

I parked the car and walked them through the hospital and down a long corridor to ICU. They remained silent the whole time, as did I. I felt like I had to keep going, or I would lose courage. I couldn't stop or say anything. I must keep going. I got them to the room where their father was surrounded by machines, IVs, and nurses. With hardly any room for us to go in, I ushered the girls to his bedside. I remember sweet Matilda, stroking his one finger that poked out of all the mess of wires and IVs.

She kept repeating, "His eyes are closed; his eyes are closed."

Ruby was frightened and didn't know what to do. She was very quiet. I looked up and saw a tear in the nurse's eye.

All I could say was, "Girls, say good-bye to your daddy. He's going to heaven. We won't see him anymore."

I heard two sweet voices say, "Good-bye, Daddy. I love you." And all they got in response was the beeping of machines.

No words can describe the pain of that day.

Grover continued to inspire and amaze me even as he exited the world. He was an organ donor and gave two kidneys to help others. The transplant organization had to keep him alive another twenty-four hours before they could remove his organs. I didn't expect to have to deal with a delay in my grief, one of the frustrations with organ donation. I couldn't take it anymore and went home to start grieving, surrounded by his and my family. I received a call that Grover passed away March 8, 2013, at the age of forty-eight, and by donating his kidneys, he saved two women with children as he left us.

Part 2
In the Twinkling: Our Time to Grieve

In the Twinkling

In the twinkling of an eye,
primrose path goes cold and gray
with the sorrow of a sigh;
my dear friend has gone away.

Troubled times of yesterday
echo in the by-and-by.
From this wicked world you stray
in the twinkling of an eye.

Not a chance to say goodbye.
If I could, what would I say?
Nothing but to sit and cry—
primrose path goes cold and gray.

Lay me down to sleep, I pray,
help me not to ponder why.
Lay aside the disarray
with the sorrow of a sigh.

Gazing up to the starlit sky,
at the cosmic vast display,
as the finch and linnet fly,
my dear friend has gone away.

In the twinkling—

Grover Mundell

For more poems, see the appendix.

The pain was fierce. It's hard enough healing on your own, but to also help two children deal with their grief at the same time is unimaginable. We were fortunate to have therapists help us, but we also helped each other. I needed my girls as much as they needed me. I had to put myself in their shoes to understand how their pain felt, so I could help them. In doing so, I was forced to feel the pain and found it helped me heal as well. It was important that I stopped to feel in those special moments of healing and that I recognized the gift of healing my girls were giving me.

I remember those special moments vividly.

"Mom," says Ruby as we enter the Dollar store, "I read in school that there are lozenges that make you feel sad. The ingredients are sugar, strawberry and something special. Do you think we could buy them at the store to help us remember Daddy?"

"I don't think that is real Ruby," I said; and then backtracking to not destroy her hope I said, "we can try it if you want." She smiles and we walk to the candy aisle, and she grabs a bag of Jolly Ranchers off the shelf.

After we check out and get back into the car, Ruby asks a few times if I want to try it and me being on an eternal diet said no a few times. I finally give in, mentally agree to be present for my child's imagination, and say "if we are going to do this, we need to park, sit in the car, and really feel it." She agrees. We each take our "lozenge."

After exploring the flavor in our mouths, Ruby says, "what do you think?" Not sure how to answer I ask her what she thinks. She smiles mischievously and says, "I asked you first."

I close my eyes, take a deep breath, and say "it reminds me of Daddy's laugh. He had a great laugh. I think of the good memories. What does it remind you of?"

She says smiling, "it reminds me of yours and Daddy's wedding, you dancing around and my cousin as the flower girl."

I pause for a moment wondering why she chose a memory that didn't include her. Had she forgotten all the memories? I smile and say, "that is my memory. What do you remember of you and Daddy?"

She says, "I remember him putting me to sleep." When I ask her what else, she responds with a moody reply, "this lozenge thing was a bad idea. I didn't know you would want to talk about feelings. Blah, Blah, Blah. Just thought you would feel it." That was my clue to end the conversation. We were entering emotional territory. I drive the car off to pick up her sister.

A few minutes later Matilda gets into the car, and Ruby offers her a lozenge. Ruby tells her it is made up of a special ingredient to allow you to feel sad and remember Daddy. Matilda says, "I think the special ingredient is tears. I taste the tears and remember."

Along the journey, we also had to deal with tough situations with peers.

One night when I got home from a long day of work and asked Ruby how her day was, she broke into tears and said, "a boy called me a weirdo because I didn't have a dad." My heart hurt, not just because of a mean name, but because it was THAT mean name.

Throughout the healing period, we had gone to therapist and have had our "team" to support us. My therapist warned me that kids have a different grieving cycle. One that dips in and out throughout their whole entire childhood feeling the same intensity at any age rather than like an adult that experiences it more intensely at the beginning and then it becomes less painful over time.

Matilda was only two-years old when we lost her father. She doesn't have many memories. She is angry. She wasn't given a memory to take with her, at least a consolation prize for me and Ruby. Matilda didn't realize what she had lost until she turned five, once the realization of permanence had set in. I noticed her starting to act in defiance and anger, similar to a two or three-year-old who is declaring their independence but with anger and hate in their eyes. I worried about her and reached out to a psychologist, play therapist and her teachers to get her the help she needed. It was her time to face grief, to work through it, to feel all that pain, so that she could get to the other side. Ruby and I had gone through it, and we wanted to support her and let he know she wasn't alone. I knew I needed to equip her with the right tools for the journey, so that she may handle the turbulence with the least amount of injuries.

I'm very lucky to be able to afford resources and have a strong community supporting us, but no matter who you are, the same work must be done. Matilda started interpreting her grief as her identity and it made her feel alone and unworthy. She began writing notes to me and her teacher saying "I am stupid. I am worthless. I want to die. I want to kill myself." Tough words for a six-year old to write and tough words for me to read. When you have kids, the grieving of death isn't over after a year, you as the surviving parent continue to deal with it day in and day out as a caregiver. Years later it hurt my heart to hear those words from my child as much as walking down the hospital corridor. In both situations, there was nothing I can do to fix it, to make it go away. I could only hold her, listen to her cries and love her.

When I went to the therapist to discuss what to do and how best to help my child, the therapist said, "Your child is associating her identity with the grief. She feels alone because she is the girl without the father. We should make sure she understands it's something that happened to her, not who she is. She isn't a *weirdo* because her father is dead, and we need to help her understand that. She is not alone. Others have lost a parent. Then, that will address her self-esteem."

So away we went and began working on it with weekly play therapy, "Girl Talk" weekly chats with me and the two girls about our feelings, one-on-ones monthly so each girl has time with me, reading books to help me and the teacher be better, empathetic listeners. Matilda's notes started to change from self-deprecation to happiness and pictures illustrating our vacation. I breathed a sigh of relief when I saw a happy note and began to see a light at the end of the tunnel.

So, when I heard that another child called my daughter a "weirdo for not having a dad," twisting a knife in the biggest wound there is, I crumbled.

But we felt it, released it, and got back up the next day.

I often panicked I wouldn't remember stories about their dad to tell my girls. Slowly the girls began living longer without him than with him in their lives, and more pressure was on me to keep his memory alive.

"I can't remember anything," Matilda cried into my shoulder. Her body shaking, and her tears dripping down her face. "What about that time you and Daddy saw the snake outside our door?" I asked. She said, "I don't remember it" in between sobs.

"What about the time Daddy pushed you on the swing?" I said. "I can't remember it," she said still hysterically crying.

I was quiet for a few seconds while I scrolled through all the memories in my head thinking to myself. *Come on there must be more memories that I can tell her about. She's forgetting. She was only two-years old when he died. This isn't fair.*

"This isn't fair," Matilda said. "I know. I know. It's not fair. I'm so sorry."

And I did the only thing I could do. I hugged her and held on.

And then the pain softened and just became a part of who we were.

The girls and I were on vacation in Los Angeles exploring the city and shopping. I allowed them to pick a few souvenirs as we shopped different stores. Matilda really wanted a ukulele she spotted at the beginning. I told her to explore more, and we could come back and get it at the end if she really wanted it.

After two days, Matilda still had her heart set on the ukulele, so we went back in the shop to buy it. It was a cheap, blue toy ukulele with flowers on it, but she loved it. I took it out of the package for her, and then she began to strum it. I had a flashback of her dad wanting to purchase a ukulele on our honeymoon in Hawaii. We were at an outdoor market with lots of artisans, and he saw it and wanted it. He ended up buying it, and we still have it today. The kids play with it now. He never learned to play it like he could play the guitar, but it was on his list to learn one day. That ukulele is very dear to the kids' hearts since it was their dad's and just the perfect size for their little bodies.

I looked down at that sweet girl playing her new, blue ukulele, and realized she was hoping the ukulele strings would provide a connection to her dad. Probably missing him on a vacation with just the three of us. Spending time with friends who had complete families with fathers and seeing all the families at the beach resort probably made her feel disconnected and missing him. I had forgotten that it may appear odd a mother with her two children vacationing at a beach, but maybe my children hadn't forgotten. I had moved on to just the three of us and all the places we could explore, but maybe Matilda wasn't there yet. She was still longing and disconnected. Her mind wandering, she strummed into the night trying to find the right tune to heal her broken heart.

The next day at the airport in one of the stores in the middle of a crowd, Matilda sat down on the floor and pulled out the ukulele that had been tucked in her backpack and played it while calling out, "daddy, daddy," confirming what I had thought. I smiled at her and asked her if she missed her dad. She smiled and nodded yes back.

It was time to catch our plane. As we walked down the airport hallway, a woman in her 20s walked up to Matilda and showed her a ukulele still in the box she had purchased and said "that's cool you have a ukulele. I bought one too!" They both smiled at each other.

And then I saw how everything was connected. These simple ukulele strings connected us to a random stranger, Matilda to her father, me to his memory, and created a deeper connection between me and Matilda.

Ruby had been begging me for a dog, and I kept pushing it off. We often visit the pet store, and I let the girls pet the animals there. They run from rabbit, to puppy to bird and back again. It keeps them entertained for an hour or so. It was getting close to Ruby's birthday month, and I told her we would visit the pet store, but not buy her one for her birthday.

Well, we spotted this adorable, furry, white miniature poodle puppy and it was game over. All three of us fell in love and within a few minutes I was buying that puppy. The girls were thrilled.

Later that night while I put Ruby in the bed, we spoke about the responsibilities of a pet. After I went through the list of what she must do, I said, "I can't believe I bought that dog." She said, "I knew you would. Daddy grants me wishes and that was one of them."

"Oh really?" I said. "What do you mean daddy grants you wishes?" "He grants me three wishes every day, and they come true. Sometimes I wish for a green light on the way to school or sometimes I wish for something at school. This time I wished for the puppy. Daddy makes them come true. And when I close my eyes really tightly sometimes he comes to me and tells me things."

"What does he tell you?" I asked. "He tells me he loves me," Ruby says.

"I'm so glad he does that," I said. "You have one amazing Daddy who loves you a lot."

And when I thought we had taken a step forward, life would make us take a step back.

"Are you really my mommy? Tell me the truth," Matilda said to me in complete seriousness as I was putting her to bed one night. I tried to hide my pain and not take it personal. "What do you mean?" I asked. "Of course I'm your mommy. I remember when you were born. You have my nose and my curly hair."

"Please tell me the truth. Are you really my mommy?" she asked again. I paused for a minute trying to understand.

In the absence of a spouse, I had hired a new au pair to help watch the girls while I worked full time. We had many au pairs, but the transition period is always tough. They usually stay a year. On the one hand, it's so great we love our au pairs from all over the world – Birte in Germany, Alejandra in

Mexico, Johana in France and now a new one Nathalia from Brazil, but on the other hand we feel the loss all over again. Matilda (as well as Ruby and I) was having to face a loss again.

"Matilda, I'm your mommy, and I will always be here for you. I know you feel sad that another au pair is gone, but we will have friends all over the world we can visit. It sounds like you are feeling scared and uncertain. Your mommy is still your mommy. The au pair is not replacing me, only helping me."

She nodded in agreement with my words and hugged me. I could feel her loneliness and it ran deep. Her pain was also my pain. I hugged her tighter hoping my words and my love would bring her comfort and security.

It wasn't easy to grieve, parent two children who had lost their father, and move our lives forward. It wasn't the best time to start a nonprofit. But if I didn't do it, then who would? If I didn't do it, then Grover's death was meaningless and I was left without hope. I needed to help others to heal and give myself (and the girls) courage and hope to move forward.

Part 3

This Special Place:
The Packaged Good Story

There Have Been Places

with porches,
stoops,
balconies,
and even large yards—
indeed entire countrysides.

There have been places
with hallways
and freeways
and train tracks
and utter emptiness.

I've had high-rise apartments
in the near north
and poolside apartments
off ASU.
There were seasons
on the couch
of a friend of a friend.
There were group houses
in beautiful California
valleys.

And crash pads
and sleeping bags
and dorm rooms
and girlfriends' places.

In Texas and Arizona,
in Chicago and in Philly,
Florida—there have been places
many roads
have led me here.

No matter.

Tonight there is a balcony.
I can see downtown Denver
over the shimmering reservoir
and a full moon,
temperature perfect,
cold beer,
comfort.

And tonight
I'm sitting out here
and taking full advantage
of this special place.

Grover Mundell

For more poems, see the appendix.

The Beginning

After Grover died, I cried many tears, in public bathrooms, at work, at home. I went to weekly therapy to ask, "Why him?" and "Why was I left?" I felt guilty; "Did I do enough?" I went through many different stages of grief: all of them, and I continue to do so.

In his book *David and Goliath*, Malcom Gladwell[1] analyzes why some people can respond to tragedy with growth and others with weakness. A lot of this he attributes to the fact that the person is forced to persist, to invent, and to chart their own way. He goes on to say almost a third of the presidents of the United States lost their fathers when they were young. They were forced to learn skills to offset the loss.

I related to Gladwell's theory in that I had to persist, that I had to grow. Now I was the only parent, so I knew I had to get in better shape, spiritually and physically. And while Grover managed our finances and his legacy well, I still needed to offset the second income that was no longer coming in. And so I persisted. I needed to develop my inner self to become a more available, empathetic parent. And so I grew. I also had some comfort knowing that if I could get my girls the tools and support for them to get through their grief, they would also persist.

To my surprise, after many months of grief, I was thriving, physically, emotionally, and mentally, but there was still a hole, a need to fulfill Grover's dying wish and help others. I knew Grover would be proud that we were surviving, but I could still remember his plea that "we needed to do more." So I began exploring what I could do to fulfill his vision. What was missing was a meaning behind Grover's death and my purpose for being the surviving spouse. Meaning and purpose would help me move forward.

I soon noticed a few children's birthday parties where the mother added a charity component, such as packing care packages for soldiers or donating money to a charity in lieu of a gift. Those mothers and their children wanted to do more, and I loved the way that children were being exposed to doing good in such a celebratory manner. Doing good wasn't a chore; it was an event.

I wondered if my business skills could develop a platform to foster such events. With my retail background, I daydreamed about a charity storefront like Build-A-Bear, but for giving. Kids would get engaged by selecting the charity of their choice; they would decorate a bag and care package filled with toiletry supplies, school supplies, and toys; get a sticker that said, "I did good"; and then take a picture and share it. As a working single mom, I wanted to remove all barriers to volunteering and make it extremely easy for families to give. Personally, I wanted to make more meaning of my life – by helping others and creating a business. And just like that, this special place, The Packaged Good, was born.

On a mission to instill in children the desire to give back while inspiring the next generation of giving, The Packaged Good provides a fun, inspirational environment where kids and community groups can decorate and personalize care packages and create craft projects for people in need. Whether it's giving to our armed forces, the elderly, the homeless, or hospitalized kids, The Packaged Good partners with vetted, reputable nonprofit organizations to allow volunteers to support causes closest to their hearts while handling all the logistics.

In the first fourteen months of opening, we hosted more than two hundred events, and children and families created twenty thousand care packages. We opened our doors to children's birthday parties, corporate events, church youth groups, temple groups, moms' nights out, neighborhood groups; we welcomed anyone who wanted to get together to do good.

So how did I, a widowed mother of two in the middle of grieving, get it up and running in less than five months, with no previous nonprofit experience? Passion sure does help. I had a drive to create Grover's legacy for my girls and to help others, to give his death meaning and purpose. Creating is also healing, and I also just love building businesses. Here is a five-step guide that lays out how I did it, so that you may too birth a beautiful nonprofit to help your community.

Step 1: Business Planning

I have done a lot of business plans in my life, from Spanx to consulting for small businesses, but I had never written a nonprofit business plan. I Googled "nonprofit business plans" and figured out which pieces were relevant to my business: competitive landscape, overview of my offering and what makes it unique, fundraising strategy, impact statement, and budget. The first part is similar to a for-profit business plan, but the differences are fundraising instead of sales and instead of ROI in terms of profit, there's an ROI in terms of impact to society. You need a way to measure that impact.

For The Packaged Good, our impact started out in terms of quantity of care packages created. For my annual estimated fundraising goal of $150,000, I estimated we could do twenty thousand care packages. We also wanted to increase volunteerism at a young age. For instance, we wanted kids to go from one to two hours of volunteer time per year to four to five hours per year.

My fundraising strategy started out with a combination of monetary donations from corporations, grants, and individuals, and in-kind items. The in-kind items (toiletries, school supplies, small toys) proved to be difficult in large volumes, and the corporate sponsorships took longer than expected, so I had to adjust the strategy. To offset what wasn't working in the fundraising strategy, I set up two layers of community involvement: Founding Families agreed to donate $5,000 a year, and members of a community Advisory Council agreed to donate $1,000 a year and their talent. I reached out to my network, and within six weeks, we had The Packaged Good funded for the first year; 30 percent of the revenue came from the community, and the remaining 70 percent came from private events and grants. I hadn't planned on this approach initially, but it was actually better: less time consuming and more sustainable. You need a great plan to get you started, but you also need to be able to react and adjust as needed. I didn't do this alone, by any means. I tapped into amazing mentors and advisors to help me come up with great solutions and spread our mission. Although it's not perfect, it's running, and we're making a difference.

While I was creating the business plan, I tested some parties out of my home. I reached out to friends to attend the first The Packaged Good care package party to create care packages for US soldiers abroad and for Children's Healthcare of Atlanta. I bought all the supplies myself: toiletry items, Ziploc bags, stickers, baby clothes, and so on. During those parties, I learned what worked and what didn't. For instance, the smaller kids needed a predesigned bag with contained areas for coloring on the card because they were scribbling all over the place. Also, I was reminded that permanent markers don't go well with younger kids.

At first, we assembled care packages that cost $20 each, which I quickly realized wasn't sustainable. We wanted to make sure we could engage as many families and children in the community as possible, and I needed to reduce the cost of an event by purchasing items in bulk and finding cheaper alternatives. Over time, we reduced our supply cost from $20 to $5.50 to $3 per care package. If not already funded from another source, we only need a $5 donation per care package from the volunteer to help us offset cost of supplies and programming. This model helped to get us up and running with a little bit of seed money. It was unique to ask a volunteer to not only donate time but also donate money. In some areas it worked better than others. For private events, where a parent or corporation sees perceived value of the event space beyond just doing good, it has been hugely successful and self-funding.

I also sent out a survey through Survey Gizmo, a free survey tool, to find out more about my target audience (parents with small children): when they wanted to volunteer and what types of activities they were interested in. I posted the link on Facebook and asked my friends in Atlanta to fill it out. While I sometimes thought like my target audience, I also learned many new things simply by asking them for input.

Once the plan was created with all the information I gathered, I presented it to several leaders in the community to get their feedback. I presented it over seventy-five times. I received lots of feedback and revised the presentation more than sixteen times before I moved forward. Once it had been challenged a few rounds, I felt like it was in a good place to take the next step. I took the criticisms with the perspective of the end goal: to make my strategy the best it could be. This is a skill to develop, and each time I presented and heard feedback, it got easier to not take it personally.

I did all this in four weeks while working part-time at Spanx and dropping my kids off in the morning and picking them up in the afternoon from school. I was inspired and started to feel like a Pistol-Packing Momma again.

Step 2: Getting a Board

I researched online and found out I needed a board in place to apply for a 501(c)(3). A 501(c)(3) is a letter from the government that grants your nonprofit tax-exempt status. Every person, foundation, and business wants a tax write-off when they donate money, so this is critical and you really must obtain a 501(c)(3) to get any large donations. I needed at least three unrelated (literally no family) people to form my board. I reached out to my friends and added people who complemented my skill set. A friend who had her own nonprofit was a great asset to get me up and running; I added a friend who was an estate attorney, accountant, and community leader; and my sister-in-law had a PhD in organizational behavior and was in human resources in large corporation. Then, I made friends with a mother who had a daughter in school with Matilda; she was very active in volunteering and wanted to get more involved. I asked her to join the board as well. Later, two colleagues who had previously worked with me at Spanx joined too. That was the group that helped me launch The Packaged Good storefront or facility.

Over time, we evolved the board and created two groups, a board of five to seven people (including myself) that had a term of two years, met more regularly, and made day-to-day decisions, and an Advisory Council of twenty community leaders, who were involved in larger strategic discussions. I am so lucky to be surrounded by amazing people who want to make a difference. Lesli, Ilana, Lydia, and Laura became the magical four (and I made five) for my board to really get the ball moving.

When choosing a board, it's important to get people who are complementary in skill set, who are passionate about your mission, and who are willing to either do some work or raise some money. It's very important for the board to have passion, since it's a volunteer position and work needs to be done, but sometimes the board gets burned out or life happens, and they find they can no longer contribute the same amount of time. It's okay to rotate them out and transition them to a new role that is a better fit (or completely transition them out, if they prefer). I had a few people who absolutely added value but needed to rotate off at some point. They remain supporters of The Packaged Good but in a different capacity.

To make the board official, there is legal paperwork and insurance. I found a board contract template online, updated it to be relevant to my organization, and had everyone sign. Bylaws, company-specific rules such as number of board members, approval process, and so on, also need to be voted on and signed by the board, and the board needs to sign a conflict of interest agreement. This form states that the board member can't receive a profit (e.g., the nonprofit can't pay a board member's consulting company a lot of money) or have some type of conflicting interest that creates a moral dilemma. LegalZoom gave me generic versions of each to use, but I also researched online and then customized both documents for my organization. To protect your board from liability, you need to secure general and board insurance, as well.

Step 3: Government Documents

The government documents section was the area I was the least comfortable with and the one that caused me a lot of anxiety. Some of the answers just aren't clear. What is your classification? Which approvals from the federal, state, county, and city level of government do you need?

I had heard about the 501(c)(3) application. I had read that a lawyer is helpful for getting the 501(c)(3), so I just used LegalZoom to help me. LegalZoom provided all the forms and layout. It does take a little longer because they take a week to get back to you on updates you need to make. In hindsight, I may have paid a little more for a lawyer to move faster. The 501(c)(3) application took me two months to finalize with the back-and-forth to LegalZoom and six weeks to get approval by the IRS. The application is about twelve pages, and there are several attachments to it. It includes information on the board, a three-year budget, overview of programs, and some marketing material.

I also found out by making many calls to the IRS that if I was soliciting more than $20,000 a year in donations, I needed to get a solicitation license from the city. Not many nonprofits know about that one; many are under the monetary threshold. Lastly, I needed a business license from the city as well (some places may need to get the business license from the county or state).

Other than the 501(c)(3), there wasn't a lot of help out there to know which legal paperwork and approvals I needed. I asked a lot of people who had started their own nonprofits. While everyone directed me to the 501(c)(3), the rest seemed more specific to the type of nonprofit business. This is where it's useful to pay a nonprofit attorney and nonprofit accountant a consultation fee to understand all that is needed. There are also community nonprofits that will provide this guidance for free, if you aren't in a hurry.

Step 4: Brand and Marketing

Finally, I got to a step that was more comfortable for me: building my own brand. This was the fun part. Thankfully, my old Spanx colleagues Barb, Beth, Maggie, and Lydia were available to help me create all the pieces and craft my story. I started out with our mission, which was to empower kids of all ages to do good, and I put together a mood board with bright pictures of art studios that evoked warm, fun feelings. From there, I worked with designers to create a logo and brand colors and bring them to life through cards, bags, worksheets, and more. Don't underestimate the importance of building your brand, and don't be shy about asking friends and family for help. You just build the brand once, and it involves a lot of soul-searching on what you want it to be and where you want it to go. It was a lot of work, and I loved it. Where we ended was so much stronger due to the help I received from friends, experts, and most importantly friends who are experts.

The brand was born complete with my mission, story, visual center, and key selling points. I then applied everything to digital communication channels: web, Facebook, Twitter, Instagram, and email. I paid a small agency $600 to create my website, based on copy I wrote that provided direction on layout and navigation, brand colors, and the logo. After researching options, I set up email with Constant Contact and Facebook directly and got help setting up the other channels. While I ran Spanx's email business, it had been a really long time since I was the one to actually send out an email. My skills had gotten a little rusty over time. I thought my old team probably got a kick out of the first email I sent, which had broken links and errors in it. It wasn't perfect, but I got it up and running. I then set up a volunteer committee and part-time staff to help me manage the channels.

I get asked a lot about social media and what small businesses or nonprofits need to do to get more engagement. After talking to many businesses, I suggest stepping back and identifying what makes the brand unique and the core brand pillars (e.g., what's your personality?). Is it service? Is it innovation? Key differentiators we wanted to communicate for The Packaged Good were:

1. It is available for kids of all ages. Many nonprofits require children to be eight years or older.

2. It engages kids through hands on arts and craft projects to give back. Doing good can also be fun.

3. It is convenient to the volunteer. We schedule a private event whenever the volunteer wants, and we have drop-in periods where a family can just drop in to do good. We are nimble to respond to crisis situations and flexible to support do-good demand on major holidays.

From a brand perspective, there are usually three to five brand pillars that make up its personality and provide filters to help make decisions if it's right for your brand. For The Packaged Good, ours are children, arts and crafts via the packaging and personalization of a gift, and our family story of channeling grieving and pain into giving. Now, every idea we have must support all the brand filters for it to become a reality. For example, while we sometimes host adult-only events, we will talk about the importance of instilling the value of giving in their kids, and we focus on family events in our marketing efforts. Instead of just packing backpacks with school supplies, we make sure to add cards from the kids and a bow or other personal detail to create a hands-on experience for all ages. Every item we bring into the facility for decoration or signage needs to make sense within our filters. The signage can't be for an adult only; we need a version for children. The brand filters guide everything we do to ensure we communicate a clear point of view and stay true to our mission: that's what the best brands do.

Once the filters and the brand personality are set, then it's easy to set up content to go out through social media channels. For instance, we highlight Do Gooders once a week, and they demonstrate how they took grief or a bad situation and channeled it into giving. Another piece of content will be about how a child is making a difference. Content needs to engage its audience to be successful. I credit the Facebook channel for growing our awareness. I posted as much as I could along with our volunteers. The news spread fast within the communities of Dunwoody and metro Atlanta.

With the help of my friend Maggie, I used my story to get initial local press. I had never done PR before, but I learned from my friend that it's really about maintaining relationships with writers. Once these relationships were set, I continued to pitch stories myself. In the first 14 months, The Packaged Good was in the local press (TV and newspaper) over fifty times. Eventually, I got press coverage for the good events and the amazing kids who did great things, but my story really helped to jump-start awareness.

Step 5: Set Up the Facility

Before I could set up my facility, I needed to expand my insurance coverage. As employees are added, workers' compensation is needed as well as volunteer insurance. I added disclaimers to our volunteer forms and to every bag to legally protect us from liability. I cut costs in many areas, but insurance, legal, and accounting were not among them. I'm a rule follower and like to have my ducks in a row. Plus, I had no experience in those areas and really leaned on expert advice.

Getting the facility set up was truly a community effort. I knew I wanted it to be local and near my house and the girls' school, so I looked for locations in Dunwoody, Georgia. Once I found the perfect location (It used to be an art studio that I took the girls to on the weekends. A comforting place where we went to heal – the girls through art and me through time. So, it only made sense that this was the perfect location), I asked the leasing agent for a temporary lease until I could prove out the concept. I wasn't sure if they would do it, but I asked. And they did. Our landlord, Regency Centers, has been amazing and extremely supportive throughout the process.

I had a friend who owned her own office furniture company, Office Creations, so I reached out to her, and she donated all the furniture to get the facility up and running (and she delivered it and set it up). My parents' pediatric office in Dunwoody, Pediatric Health Center, donated old cabinets that a painter painted for free with bright colors of paint donated by a local paint store. A local company, Jeckil Promotions, donated supplies and printed our bags and cards for us at a low cost. Things just lined up. The greater Atlanta and Dunwoody community responded and wanted to do good, but I also got support throughout the United States: monetary donations and words of encouragement.

Those five steps (and a whole lot of community support) got me from concept to a creation of a nonprofit company in less than five months. We learned and adapted along the way, but we didn't let perfection or navigating new territory get in the way of progress.

Starting a nonprofit is tough work. A nonprofit requires you to wear multiple hats, including fundraiser and program provider. For anyone who wants to start a nonprofit, I suggest you have two partners: a business person for running the operations and fundraising and a programming person who is great at delivering excellence in programs. Without both sides, it's difficult to scale and sustain the model. I'm also an advocate for partnerships and mergers. We're all trying to do good; why not collaborate to make a bigger impact?

After all the hours and effort I put into building the business, I recommend to anyone who wants to start their own nonprofit to first look and see if you can be a program under an existing nonprofit. This allows you to focus more of your time on doing good than administrative, business, and fundraising efforts. If you are adamant to start your own nonprofit, use my five steps and buckle down for a tough and challenging ride. I'm glad I did it, but it was a lot of work and effort.

The Impact

The process of building the company was fun for me. I have always loved building businesses, but I didn't realize the joy and healing giving would bring. It gave me a purpose bigger than myself, and seeing the impact gave me a sense of fulfillment like no other. It made me smile again.

The girls felt very much a part of it. They are very artistic, so they helped me decorate the facility and test out all the supplies and process. They ran "Do Good" stations within the facility and chose to celebrate their birthday at The Packaged Good. One day, when I talked to the girls about what they wanted to do when they get older, Matilda said, "I'm going to run The Packaged Good."

My kids weren't the only ones receiving joy. Our care packages brought joy around the world. A soldier wrote us, telling us he received his care package all the way in China and how much it meant to him and others. He was honored to be serving the little girl who wrote the card.

Espere Counseling Group brought some of our bags with them to Haiti, and they told us, "Toiletries are like gold in Haiti. They have nothing. What you did was amazing."

What I most enjoyed about the whole process was seeing the light turned on, seeing the energy change in both the giver and the receiver. It was a love exchange. Both lights were getting brighter. What a gift to give a child: awareness that they have the gift to give at any age. It's empowering. Can you imagine what impact it makes on a four-, five-, or six-year-old to know they have the gift of kindness and the power to make a difference in the world today?

A group of The Packaged Good families went to visit a local nursing home. Fifteen kids ran around the hallways of the very bland, sterile nursing home, giving out care packages and smiles. It adds so much energy to the nursing home, and the residents can feel it. I saw a three-year-old sit on the lap of an elderly blind woman, who was sitting in a wheelchair, and hold her hand. One of the elderly ladies in her room visited by the kids told them, "I will hold onto this card until it rots. It's the nicest thing anyone has ever done for me."

At another visit at an assisted living facility in Atlanta, an elderly woman told me she was having "the worst holiday ever" when we came to visit her and other residents on Christmas Day, but our visit turned it around for her. "This week has been depressing," she said to me. "There was no one around. No joy. You made my holiday by coming to visit today."

I was also able to see the ripple effect of giving with my own eyes. Bhaumi, a girl who was thirteen years old, came to me to volunteer. She attended an event and raised over $1,300 for The Packaged Good by setting up a bake sale and a pay-for-play game at her school. She felt empowered, her light got brighter, and she wanted to do more. Then she used her videography passion to create educational videos for us, which we still use today. And she kept going and doing more for other nonprofits: serving on children's boards, hosting events, and doing more videos for other nonprofits. She got her sister and her parents more involved. It was amazing.

And then there's Harrison, a twelve-year-old boy, who came to help me at a care package booth I had set up at Temple Emanu-El, where I am a member, and he took over the booth and helped other kids make care packages for people in need. He was empowered, his light got brighter, and he felt good giving. He wanted to do more. He started running events for

The Packaged Good. With his Bar Mitzvah money, he bought the biggest donation of toiletry supplies we've ever received, over three pallets worth of supplies. He joined my Advisory Council (the only kid to do so) and now helps us make strategic decisions (and boy, do the other adults in the room listen when he speaks). He went on to take a social action role at Temple Emanu-El and keeps on giving.

When the tooth fairy left a five-dollar bill for my daughter, Matilda, she quietly tucked it away. And with no prompting from me, she brought it with her to The Packaged Good and dropped it in the donation jar. All she said was, "Mom, it's more important that I help others who have nothing, when I already have so much."

Yesterday, as I walked out the door to watch kids from an orphanage choir perform, Ruby handed me five dollars out of her wallet to give to them.

The energy and conversation around me has changed. It is now about how we can help and how we can do more to make a difference. I also feel a deeper connection in all my interactions.

The first advertising video I did for The Packaged Good, I was holding back tears the whole video, so I'm not smiling at all. My kids tease me that I look like a deer in headlights. I say in the video, "This is really exciting," but I'm frowning. It was so hard for me to do. I didn't want to talk about what I had lost. But I had to talk about it to heal and explain why The Packaged Good is so important to me and the larger community.

There were days when I was down, sad, or frustrated, but when I spent time visiting others and giving to those in need, I felt good again. I would share my story and allow myself to be vulnerable, and someone would always share theirs back. It provided an instant connection and empathy between us. I found purpose and happiness when I shared my story. It made me see that the tragedy was also a blessing. If I shared it, it turned into a gift. If I held it to myself, it was a tragedy.

I remember meeting a woman who was just like me: had a degree, two kids, about my age. Our stories diverged because she ended up getting addicted to a drug; she ultimately lost her husband and kids and wasn't allowed to interact with them. I can't even imagine the horror of it. She now had gotten herself clean, but the state hadn't allowed her to get her kids back yet. When I told her my story of loss and pain, she told me hers. We connected.

I remember her saying, "I can't imagine what you've been through."

"I can't imagine what you've been through," I said back. Giving felt good, and it brought us closer together.

With all the world's issues, I found the community was hungry for a way to give back and connect to others in today's busy, always digitally connected, but disconnected lifestyle. In the first year, The Packaged Good was in the news and TV. We got voted "Best Nonprofit" at a local nonprofit's, Pebble Tossers', annual event by teens and kids in the community. I spoke at Fortune 500 companies, small businesses, schools, temples, and churches.

For Martin Luther King (MLK) Day, The Packaged Good hosted an event with two local nonprofits, Homeless at Heart and the Community Assistance Center, to make care packages for local homeless people. Over fourteen hundred people came out to do good throughout the day. It was insane. My little nonprofit went viral, and over fourteen hundred people showed up. I looked around and saw people of all races and religions joined together, making care packages for people in need in our own community. It had brought us together. It made us stronger as a community. Giving made us all feel good, and giving connected us. We made close to four thousand care packages that day and sent out positive energy and love in our own community. It was bittersweet to see Grover's dream realized on MLK Day. When I met Grover, he had a MLK poster hanging up in his condo. His voice has been a consistent guide throughout.

The community has consistently come together to support others throughout natural disasters: Haiti, Louisiana, and most recently Texas, Florida and the islands. At our packing event for Texas, we filled up donations in a twenty-six-foot truck, and over eight hundred people came out to pack care packages. The Packaged Good was the platform that allowed the community to come together to do good.

The Benefits of Doing Good

After seeing the impact of giving on people emotionally and physically, I began to research this idea of giving as a healing therapy, and I found plenty of support. In the *Journal of Economic Psychology* in 2014,[2] Baris Yörük found that giving to others reduced stress and strengthened the immune system. A 2008 study by Harvard Business School[3] professor Michael Norton and colleagues found that giving money to someone else lifted participants' happiness more than spending it on themselves.

According to a study from the University of California, Berkeley,[4] people who were fifty-five and older who volunteered for two or more organizations were 44 percent less likely to die over a five-year period than those who didn't volunteer.

When researchers from the National Institutes of Health[5] looked at the functional MRIs of people who gave to various charities, they found that giving stimulates the mesolimbic pathway, which is the reward center in the brain and creates what is known as the "helper's high."

According to the *Journal of American Medical Association* in 2013,[6] volunteer group of students that spent one hour per week volunteering over ten weeks had lower levels of inflammation and cholesterol and lower BMIs than those who didn't volunteer.

Teenagers who participated in volunteer activities on their own had 11 percent fewer illegal behaviors between the ages of eighteen and twenty-eight than teenagers who did not volunteer; 31 percent fewer arrests; and 39 percent fewer convictions, according to a University of Iowa study in 2017. "Adolescence is a formative period during which major moral and emotional development occurs, so self-empowering experiences like volunteering may provide a sense of social responsibility, self-worth, and happiness that helps in moral development," says Shabbar Ranapurwala, the study's lead author, who is a member of the faculty at the UI College of Public Health and at the University of North Carolina at Chapel Hill.[7]

My Jewish upbringing supported this as well. Tikkun HaNefesh, healing of your own soul, Tikkun Olam, repairing the world, and Tzedekah, helping others through service and monetary means, are core Jewish values. I found the more good I was doing, the more I felt connected to my Jewish roots. Serving others can be found at the core of every religion and the higher level of self.

Giving was the final puzzle piece we needed to move our family forward and to heal our broken hearts. Did Grover know that his vision for doing good was also giving his family the gift of healing itself?

A year after The Packaged Good was created, Father's Day was approaching, so I asked the girls what they wanted to do. They thought a minute and then Ruby responded with, "Let's throw a party for others who have lost their father. Let's give to others on Father's Day."

I hope Grover is at peace, knowing his wish came true. The seeds he planted have blossomed, and they are some Pistol-Packing Mommas.

Me in my Pistol Packing Momma dance outfit, age 5

Me and my little brother Stan, age 8 and 5.

Our wedding day - May 20, 2006 - in Grand Junction, Colorado.

Ruby and Matilda combing daddy's hair in the hospital.

Me, Grover and Matilda two months before Grover died.

We did it!
The grand opening of
The Packaged Good.

Delivering the bags to a
local assisted living facility.

Ruby and her friend proud of
their artistic gifts.

An example of our
care packages.

Part 4
Carry On: Ten Lessons Learned to Grow through Pain

Once I'm Dead

Once I'm dead
and gone,
my girls will carry on
my name,
my blood,
my dreams, my hopes, my love

Because they
are everything to me,
and I'll say
the same
to anyone:
it's all about family.

When I'm dead,
don't cry
or compose a sad goodbye,
because I
have lived
to see my life completed by
my girls—
my world
is complete.

It's all about family.

Matilda you
have my heart.
Ruby you're my art,
and all I mean
by that is that I love you.

When I'm dead
and gone,
my girls will carry on.

Grover Mundell

For more poems, see the appendix.

I am so proud to have created something beautiful out of all the pain the girls and I had gone through. It's a way for them to remember their father, a way for them to channel their pain. It really made me think; if such beauty can come out of pain, then we shouldn't fear pain. We should not seek it but embrace it if we happen upon it. If we can overcome it, if we can feel it and transform from it, we can create something beautiful. It was empowering.

As I reflect back to think about how far I've come and what I created out of a tragedy, I realize that experiences from my early years made me more resilient, open, and adventurous. Lessons in adulthood helped to develop my capabilities, and my tragedy made me more curious, vulnerable, and aware, giving me the confidence and strength to propel me forward. And maybe the most important, I had a supportive community, friends, and family. This combination not only allowed me to thrive but increased my growth. The following ten lessons I learned throughout my life helped me to get on the path for success and fulfillment.

1. Get Tough

I grew up with three brothers: two older and one younger. Hanging with the boys constantly, I had to be tough. My older brothers found it hilarious to play tricks on me when I was little. One time, they put eggs under the mat at the front door and rang the doorbell. I came to answer it and found crackling under my feet and giggling around the corner. Another time, they made me a "delicious" milkshake, consisting of tabasco sauce, ketchup, chocolate, and other secret ingredients. After drinking it, I promptly vomited it up; not surprisingly, it took me twenty years to get up the courage to try another milkshake. I would get so mad, I would pack my bags and run away from the house at five years old. We lived in a small town, and I actually got pretty far before someone brought me home.

Most days, I'd play with my brothers in the yard. We'd build forts, play tag, and roam around the neighborhood. My claim to fame (in our household anyway) in childhood was karate kicking my younger brother through my bedroom door. He was my best playmate but also my worst enemy. My older brother, Michael, was "babysitting" us (which means talking on the phone with his girlfriend while he was in the same house) while my parents were at work. Stan, my younger brother, wouldn't leave my room. He tended to be really stubborn (some things never change). I got so mad, I let out an animalistic sound at the top of my lungs and ran at him. Somehow, I managed to get my chubby eleven-year-old body up in the air and kick him with both legs. Stan didn't know what had hit him as he got crashed through my door. I felt like a little red-headed Chuck Norris. I was pretty proud of my defensive move.

I also had defensive moves on the court. Basketball (and a few years of softball, tennis, and cross country) guided and defined most of my life from an early age through college at Emory University. I played competitive basketball five or six days per week year-round for ten years. Competitive sports require a high level of mental toughness. When you think you can't run one more sprint, you must. When your team is behind, you must elevate yourself to come back. Before every game, you should connect to your inner zone for peak performance. I had years of training to do things beyond my physical capability. I learned to will myself to go further and to adjust my attitude and energy for a higher level of performance.

My dad would drop me at a gym on a rougher side of town, where many guys would come to play pickup ball in the summers. I would hang out with one of my teammates, and we would play most of the day. I definitely stood out, being an affluent, red-headed Jewish girl in the gym, but we all had basketball in common. I am also naturally introverted, but I had a huge level of self-confidence with basketball. I had no problem being cocky and leaving my hands up in the air after I drained a three-pointer in a taller, stronger guy's face. Imagine a trash-talking, three-point-shooting, red-headed white girl.

I was fortunate to grow up mentally and physically tough, but I also continued to challenge myself. I have run multiple half-marathons and a Tough Mudder, a fourteen-mile obstacle course that is set up for Navy SEALs in my adulthood. Starting a business also requires toughness and is definitely a marathon and not a sprint. Writing this book while having a marketing job, running a nonprofit, and raising two kids requires toughness. Just being a parent makes you tough, as well. My kids have literally taken me down a few times. It's good to get knocked out and get back up again. It makes you stronger, more persistent, and able to persevere.

Then when you do get knocked down in an unimaginable way, you can rise up.

2. Learn and Practice Empathy

In fourth grade, I remember doing my first real caring act. There was a girl in the class who was very poor, and her clothes were always dirty and ragged. Her hair was cut extremely short and was never brushed. The kids at school made fun of her, and it seemed like she never bathed. I couldn't believe that her parents wouldn't (or couldn't) help her. I made my first care package, filling a shoe box with new toiletries out of my home to bring to her at school. I never told my parents or my friends. It was just the right thing to do. Not liking much conflict and being introverted, I gave the shoe box full of soap, toothpaste, a brush, and shampoo to my teacher and asked her to give it to my classmate. I didn't want to make either of us feel uncomfortable, but the teacher pulled both of us out of the classroom and handed the girl my care package and told her I made it for her. I awkwardly smiled, and the girl thanked me. I often think of that day and hope she was able to perceive the package as an act of love and not of judgment or disapproval. I believed she deserved more.

I was empathetic at a young age, and I believe most kids have this innately, but as I got older, I wasn't very good at it. I got busy with work and life, and so inwardly focused on improvement that I didn't think about how others felt. I remember after an employee resigned from my team, she mentioned one of the reasons she left was because I didn't remember her birthday. That lesson was tough, but it reminded me to take the time to understand my colleagues and learn what's important to them. You may run over people and get the results you want, but it's not sustainable. To be a good manager (or a good parent), you can't just have empathy; you need to practice it. I have found that simply taking my team to lunch a couple times per year to get to know them personally makes all the difference to them and their career. Not by itself, of course, but it opens to deeper understandings. We learn what motivates each other and what's going on in each other's lives.

After experiencing a loss, empathy became easier for me. I wanted to know what was really going on in someone's life. I understood that a woman could be presenting to a room full of people and appear okay, but she could have just lost her husband a month earlier. Lives are deep, and most interactions barely scratch the surface. Over time, as I met more and more people with stories of pain, I began to realize that many of us carry pain with us and want acknowledgment of it from others. It allows us to release a portion of the pain and move on, each time with a bit less.

Being more empathetic allowed me to connect deeper with others and find solutions to help people in the community. Still, I find that I must deliberately remind myself to practice it: to hug my girls when they are sad and I am in a hurry, to ask colleagues how they are doing and how their weekend was, even when I'm close to a deadline, and to not take a slight personally because someone may have had a bad day.

3. Be Open and Adventurous

I grew up in a series of smallish cities in Georgia. My father was a pediatrician who loved helping kids feel better, but he was Goldilocks when it came to deciding where to live. My childhood consisted of getting to know new people every few years, and I was often asked if my father was in the military. Nope, he was just trying to find the perfect porridge for his family. By the time I reached twelfth grade, I had attended seven different schools.

I had to make new friends every two years, learn new schools, new houses, and new environments. I met all types of people and became adaptable to new situations and adept at fitting in wherever I went. This made it easier for me later in life when I moved to New York City, San Francisco, and Denver for work and new adventures. It made it easier to try new careers from advertising to brand strategy to digital marketing to sales to e-commerce to nonprofits. It made it easier for me to work with all types of people and learn from people very different from me. I'm still introverted, but dang it, at least I'm adaptable.

When I moved to San Francisco in 2001, I had planned on getting a job with a tech company, but it was soon after the tech bubble burst, and I couldn't land a job. I decided to work temporarily at a luxury lingerie store. I learned whatever I could about retailing and fashion. When I later interviewed for Spanx, they told me one of the reasons they considered me was because I had lingerie experience; who could have known? Be open to where the adventure may take you and enjoy the experiences along the way.

With The Packaged Good, I jumped into a new industry with no background in nonprofit corporations. I viewed it as a learning experience rather than being scared to fail. And like everything I do, I had to jump in all the way. If you view life decisions as learning experiences, then they are less scary. There's no failing, only learning with a chance of success.

Sara Blakely talks about how her father always asked her, "What did you fail at today?" Changing perspective on how we see failure allows us to take more risks. And in this case, "learning" is just productive failure. Be open to learning.

4. Build a Support System

I can't emphasize how important a support system is to your health and success. They lift you to higher levels, and they support you when you are down. I was privileged to be born into the start of my support system, and for that I am very grateful. My parents and brothers and later my sisters-in-law played a huge part in who I am today. My father coached me in basketball when I was younger and guided me to Emory University, his alma mater. My brother Louis advised me to pursue a degree in economics when I wasn't sure of my direction. He helped me get my first job out of school and helped me on most of my career and job decisions as a mentor. Louis is still the first person I call when I need advice about my career. I even worked for him for five years at his start-up in New York City.

My oldest brother Michael hired me to help him with research at his law firm; many times, he gave me a place to live and any support I needed to get on my feet again. My younger brother Stan was one of my best friends growing up and also roomed with me in New York City. We had many discussions about the purpose of life and what makes me happy. He helped me to become more introspective. My sisters-in-law Kristi, Lori, and Angie surrounded me with love and support over the years and nurtured me when I needed it most. My mom helped all my dreams come true, whether it was physically moving me (she is one strong lady!) or helping solve a problem. When Grover died, I could lean on my family whenever I needed extra support. My father and my brothers stepped up and were male role models to my girls. They took them on dates and adventures, and even taught them to ride their bikes.

Beyond my family and friends, my mentors provided new opportunities for me, believed in me, and supported me. I was so lucky to work for great thought leaders and business minds like Joey Reiman and Brian Hankin in marketing and advertising, and Sara Blakely and Laurie Ann Goldman at Spanx. All four of these mentors are now involved in my nonprofit in some way: either as sponsors or serving on the Advisory Council.

My girlfriends have also played a huge role, even beyond good laughs and emotional support. They are donors and volunteers, and some even helped edit this book. My support system is what allowed me to start The Packaged Good in less than five months and fund it for the first year within six weeks. It made all the difference to have people surrounding me who believed in me, who shared my vision, and who took action to support me.

Don't underestimate the power of asking for help and leaning on your community, and make sure you are giving your time and support to others as well. We all move forward together. We all help each other.

Make sure to only surround yourself with others you admire, who contribute to the greater good of propelling people forward. Those are the keepers for your support system. But also make time and room for others who need your help.

5. Prioritize for Impact

Throughout my life, I have worked or consulted at start-ups and high-growth companies. In all these environments, you are understaffed and pressed for time. I constantly must find ways to do more with less. My mantra at Spanx was "prioritize for impact." I ran a fairly sizeable business with a full-time internal team of eight. I learned to constantly refocus my team on the most important things, so they wouldn't get overwhelmed with too many things and get nothing done well. We focused on initiatives that had major impact instead of fifty things with minor impact and mediocre results. I also learned this from my brother Michael. When I was in my twenties, I whined to him about how I couldn't get it all done at one of my jobs. He said to me, "You don't have to do everything. Just do a few things well."

Plenty of people can point out areas of The Packaged Good I need to improve (and many have). I get lots of good ideas from this input, but I also get many ideas that I must weed out. As a small nonprofit trying to make a big impact, we ruthlessly prioritize because we can't do it all. In fact, we can only do a few things really well, so we should pick things that really matter. That's how we produce disproportionate impact for our donors and volunteers. Many times, I see people spiraling or blocked from trying to do it perfectly or doing too many things, and nothing makes an impact. Sometimes, I see that person in the mirror and have to recall my brother's teaching.

There are a few options to getting to the answer faster:

1. Research it, and if a lot of people say the same thing, you know what to do. If you follow Gary V, the social entrepreneur guru, he says, "Google is your best tool, and it's free."

2. Pay for expert advice (I recommend this in legal, accounting, and insurance areas).

3. Meet with people who have done it before. When I was filling out my 501(c)(3) application, I met with several founders of nonprofits to pick their brains before I started.

4. Ask smart people to help you get to an answer.

It's that simple to get to the answer faster, but you must take action.

6. Take Action

I like to analyze things and began life as a bit of a perfectionist, which kept me scared and lacking confidence at an early age. I had to get to the point where I felt comfortable not knowing all the answers and the end result before I started. I had to just start and then figure things out as I went. Working at Spanx and growing my career at other start-ups helped me gain the confidence to make progress toward a goal without having all the answers. When I launched the Europe e-commerce business for Spanx, there were numerous steps that I had never done before. I had to put my best plan together and start, use my strengths, and trust my ability to course correct as needed. I wasn't going to know all the answers, and no amount of preparation would eliminate all the issues.

Now, getting things done is what I do really well. I will say I'm going to do something, and it's done before I have a chance to question my decision. I launched my nonprofit five months after coming up with the idea. I wrote this book in three months. It may not always be perfect (sorry about that), but I do get things done.

If you've heard of agile development, this is pretty much my approach applied generally. With traditional waterfall development, technology teams were taking so long to develop that by the time software came out, the program was obsolete. With agile development teams, there is a general direction and vision, but software is delivered in highly iterative fashion with short-term planning horizons. Software would be out quicker and in the hands of users, and it could then be fixed quicker. This action and learning orientation is the right approach in today's busy, ever-changing world. Have a strategy, get it launched and then tweak it. Learn from mistakes.

7. Go Inside (with Help from Outside)

You can have all the success in the world, but if you don't understand yourself or your emotions, you will never be fulfilled. I needed help understanding myself (and I'm still working on it), so I spent a lot of time in therapy and writing. Reflection is important, and I take the time to reflect every day through writing, taking a meditative bath, taking a walk, or talking to my therapist. I'm a big proponent of therapy, and I always come to my sessions with three things I'm working through. It could be understanding a barrier to success in an area of my life, resolving a parenting dilemma, or navigating a difficult relationships or grief. Processing my thoughts with a therapist helps me get to the heart of the issue and how I feel about it. When Grover died, therapy opened the door for me to learn more about myself.

Children are mirrors to ourselves, and if we pay attention, we can learn a lot from them. One particular conversation with my girls clicked with me and changed me. It had been a long day. Trying to parent alone while working is tough (I might have mentioned that). My girls started fighting in the backseat of the car while I was trying to work out some ideas in my head. Of course I wanted two tired little girls to be quiet while I thought. Instead, the yelling quickly escalated to fighting each other with elbows and jabs. Then one started crying, and the other started screaming. Driving in Atlanta traffic, I lost it and yelled back at them to be quiet. I hate it when I discipline the kids for screaming by screaming. It's so much harder to parent without fear. It requires a higher level of emotional awareness and energy, and I was on empty.

Once we got home, I was seething from two girls annoying me plus my own reaction. I just wanted to stay in a negative place and think about how difficult it is being a single parent and what a bad hand I had been dealt.

Then when we got home, Ruby said, "I'm sorry, and I was frustrated with Matilda, but I shouldn't have yelled or hit her."

She took the high road, and in doing so, she released me from my negativity with those words. A moment earlier, I had thought, *My kids are brats and parenting is so hard,* only for that thought to be instantly replaced with *My child is more emotionally mature than I am.* I'm still pouting, and she's ready for forgiveness and to move on. It amazed me how quickly she transitioned her emotions.

A few minutes later, we were jumping on the trampoline, holding hands and laughing, and it dawned on me that I had just experienced a journey of emotion within such a short time frame, guided by my child. To move from emotion to emotion, it was critical that I let the previous emotion go. She helped me with that. As an adult, we want to hide or hold on to those emotions. We have a bad day or a good day. It's one emotion for the day, maybe longer. Not three emotions in an hour. Feel it. Release it. Move on.

Starting a business is a roller coaster of emotion. I needed to remind myself that I may feel defeated and sad today, and it was okay to feel it, but tomorrow will be another day. I had to be okay asking for help and be vulnerable with my insecurities: one of many lessons about myself that I've learned from observing and listening to my children.

It's important that we continue to develop our inner selves as we focus on developing our outer selves. It's how one can see the beauty in a tragedy. It's how one can have compassion and understanding during conflict. It's the path to fulfillment and happiness.

I will continue to work on this skill, and even most recently, have participated in inner development workshops through a place in Buckhead called Vanda, led by Vanda herself, a healer and guide for inner development. The more you work on the inside, the more you have to give to the outside.

8. Allow Yourself to be Vulnerable and Ask for Help

What's more vulnerable than a widow and kids who lost their spouse and father? Pretty much fell into this one. Losing Grover made it okay for me to be vulnerable, but it was still so hard to keep my walls down and be vulnerable around others. In her book *Daring Greatly,* Brene Brown[8] writes that the path to greatness requires one to learn to be vulnerable. I completely agree. Growing up, I wanted to hide my imperfections and felt shame with my mistakes and flaws. After Grover died, I cared less about appearing perfect. It naturally put me in an ongoing vulnerable state. It was a hard transition to always need help, but once I accepted it, vulnerability opened many doors for me. I started even asking for help on a large scale through social media: "People, here's where I need help." And guess what? When I asked specifically for what I needed, people responded. I needed furniture for The Packaged Good; someone donated it. I needed advice about the logo; someone would recreate it better than the original. Shoot, four people are editing this book to help me. All I have to do is ask. It was eye-opening. It really is that simple. Of course, you need a network that believes in your objectives, but they still aren't mind readers. In the nonprofit world, you must be willing to ask for what you need.

One of my most vulnerable states happened during our Martin Luther King event. As more and more people came in through the doors, I realized I stink at event planning. I needed help. I pride myself in figuring things out, but that event was pretty chaotic. That's when I reached out to the board and said we needed to bring in an executive director. I'm not the right the person for it. I am a great marketer (I did get fourteen hundred people to the event) but not a great event planner. It's hard to admit something like that, but I believe The Packaged Good will now grow bigger and better with someone who can do a better job than I can.

I get asked to speak to organizations, schools, and corporations. After I give a speech, I usually get a handful of people who come up to me wanting my advice on business, marketing, or nonprofits. Sometimes, it's not clear what they are wanting from me.

I often have to tell them, "Be clear in your ask. I'm willing to help you. I love helping people. But I don't know what it is that you are asking for my help on."

It's important that you know what you want, as simple as that sounds. Spend time writing out what you want, what help you need to get there, and ask for it. It's okay to say that you are exploring an area and just need to learn before you have a clear ask. I know I've done that many times.

Talking to different people with different perspectives will help you get to your answer. Be vulnerable and ask for what you need, but first do the inner work to know what it is that you need.

9. Be Curious

I have spent periods in my life being scared to ask questions, limited by my own insecurities. Somehow, Grover's death hit a reset button with me on this trait. These rules I followed didn't keep him alive or stop me from getting hurt. I started questioning why I was doing anything and everything. I was always a quick study with research and could get to many answers quickly. But I must temper my propensity to take action with allowing for exploration. Action does not always have to be linear, and I have allowed myself permission to go where curiosity takes me.

Being curious allowed me to see different perspectives and to pave new paths.

I love the story about the brisket. A daughter notices, over the years, that her mother cuts the end off the brisket and puts it in a large pan that would have fit the entire brisket. One day, the daughter decides to ask the mother why she does this.

The mother says, "I don't know. My mother always did it."

The daughter then goes to her grandmother and asks her why she cuts the end off the brisket. The grandmother says, "This pan I have is too small to fit the brisket."

I was going through life, unnecessarily cutting brisket, and I hadn't been curious enough to ask why I did the things I did or why others did the things they did. As an innovator and entrepreneur, you are constantly curious and asking why things are done the way they are today and seeking a better solution. An entrepreneur doesn't accept the answer, "Because that's the way we've always done it."

As I moved up in the corporate ladder, I also realized that leaders don't have expertise in every department. The best leaders ask the best questions, so they have the information they need to make an educated decision. You gain a lot more confidence as your ability to ask important questions improves. Being curious, similar to asking for help, may appear like weakness at times because you are revealing you don't have all the answers.

But you know what asking lots questions also gave me? The realization that most people don't have the answers.

10.   Make Time to Give and Express Gratitude

Let's face it: We're all busy. We crave more time. We think volunteering is a luxury item that is done a few times per year. We check the box and say to ourselves, "Good job, you covered helping people this year." But what we have forgotten, or maybe never knew, is that giving is good for your soul. It's good for your health. It's good for your emotional state.

Giving to others should be thought of like exercising, brushing your teeth, or meditating. It's part of self-care. Volunteering and helping others can improve so many areas of your life.

I can't tell you how many times I've said "volunteer" as the answer to someone's problem. Just last night, my friend was telling me she was concerned her daughter had low self-esteem because she hadn't found the thing she was good at.

I said, "She should volunteer. Let's put together a plan. Have her set up tea parties at the nursing home."

A friend was recently diagnosed with a tough disease, and she said she needed help out of her depression.

I said, "Volunteer; what's your passion?"

She went to volunteer at a home for abused and battered women, and it changed her attitude and perspective.

The activity director at a nursing home called me and told me she was worried about some of the residents who had lost hope, had lost purpose, and were depressed.

I said, "Let's figure out how they can volunteer."

They made hundreds of peanut butter and jelly sandwiches for another nursing home and felt empowered by what they did. Now they want to do more.

Parents have said to me that their kids are spoiled and don't realize how lucky they are. My response: "Have them volunteer."

I have a friend who overanalyzes his life and constantly worries about things he's done. I told him, "Volunteer to get a new perspective."

People who have recently retired often don't know what to do with their life. Volunteer.

Moved to a new city and having trouble making friends? Volunteer.

I can go on and on, but you get the idea.

In addition to volunteering, be kind to people. Actually, set goals around being kind. Ask yourself at the end of the day, "How many compliments and thank yous did I give out today? Can I double that tomorrow?"

When my girls were younger, I watched the video *1, 2, 3 Magic*[9]. The video taught parents how to discipline better to get desired results with children. One thing they teach is to compliment the child frequently throughout the day to offset criticism. It made me realize that I was only pointing out things my children were doing wrong and taking for granted the things they were doing right. I needed to express gratitude to my children for things I did appreciate that they were doing. Think of all the amazing thoughts you have about your kids that you never share with them. I have tried my best to communicate to them my love and admiration, not just the teachings and criticisms that go with parenting. The same things go for all your relationships. Make sure you say it.

Did you thank your husband for taking out the trash or for putting the kids to bed last night? I sure wish I could do that. Do you realize how lucky you are? Are you letting everyone around you know what you appreciate about them? How about your kids? Let's shoot for five compliments for every criticism you give your kid. How does that change the dynamic around for you? Do you find the more compliments you give and the more gratitude you express, the more joy you find in your life? You better believe it. Kindness is the best drug out there.

Gratitude is something I constantly work on and try to remember. It's not natural to me. I forget, and I need to remind myself to do it more. When I do practice it, I'm much happier.

Yes, we want to help other people, but we all need help. We all need healing. We all need purpose. And I have learned that as people are closer to the end of their life, they will want to make sure they have made a difference, had an impact on the world, given meaning to their life.

But for each of us, let's remember, channeling grief, sorrow and pain into giving to others truly heals the heart, the soul, and the world.

Part 5
My Happy Place: A Guide to Giving Back

My Happy Place

I wondered in that instant why
a sudden smile my face revealed
For just as I thought I'd die
from wind sprints on the practice field,
was worn and wary grasping for air,
when time stood still as I left it there,

Out of my body from time ahead
the practice and pain for years I'd yearn
I caught my wind and raised my head.
I drank the pain. I felt the burn.
Regaling the feeling I tried to remain
and capture the moment to live again.

At that point in time I couldn't know
of the benefits that would come to me
as this day became a long ago,
A milestone epiphany,
When I ran like the wind and much to my health
and much on account of wisdom's wealth.

See how it waves from out of the blue,
the sudden smile across my face,
a transcendental rendezvous?
I think it's called my happy place.
It flashes in my inner eye.
I'm back there running head up high.

Grover Mundell

For more poems, see the appendix.

I hope you have connected with my story, benefited from my lessons learned, and now realize the importance of giving for you. My lessons learned are universal and apply to anyone wanting to grow as an individual, and I hope they help you to do so. While I channeled my grieving into creating a nonprofit and immersing myself into the world of philanthropy, you can get the same benefit by simply incorporating giving into your lifestyle. By just being a loving, caring individual you make a positive impact on the world. You don't have to start your own nonprofit. There are plenty out there; they need volunteers and talent.

When I started The Packaged Good, it opened the door to a whole new world of philanthropy and to people who gave their time and energy to do good. At the start of The Packaged Good, I was fortunate enough to meet Jennifer Guynn, co-founder and executive director of Pebble Tossers, a youth development organization and family volunteering resource that connects youth and families with fun, age-appropriate service projects throughout metro Atlanta. Our organizations work closely together to make a difference and empower youth in Atlanta through programming, volunteer opportunities, and events.

In this section of the book, Jen and I partnered to come up with fifteen ways for you (and your kids) to give back today anywhere you live, a list of our favorite charities in the Atlanta area, and Jen's guide to volunteering. Don't wait; we have made it convenient and easy for you to give and make a difference immediately. I hope my story has inspired you to do more, not just for others, but for yourself. If you still need help, contact The Packaged Good (thepackagedgood.org) or Pebble Tossers (pebbletossers. org). The Packaged Good will accept all these gifts and distribute them to our neighbors in need, you can drop them directly to one of our favorite charities listed at the end of this section, or you can drop them off to your local charity. You can also check Pebble Tossers' website for contact information on any of these nonprofits or browse their twelve cause areas to discover new nonprofit organizations.

Pick an activity and then tell us what you did at #thepackagedgood #pebbletossers.

1. Use Kind Words and Actions

Say "thank you" and "you're welcome" or give a compliment. Try giving out ten compliments in one day. Write a note of gratitude for five people you want to thank and mail it to them. It's that easy to make a difference.

2. Make Sandwiches (or Complete Lunches)

Provide sandwiches or complete lunches. Peanut butter and jelly are fine; however, the preferred sandwich is ham or bologna on white or wheat bread with mustard (no mayo). Add each of the following to make it a complete lunch: a sweet snack, a salty snack, a bottle of water, piece of fruit, and a Happy Day Note.

All items should be placed in a plastic grocery bag or a tote (typically the homeless person will reuse this bag to carry personal items) If you are making multiple lunches, place ten complete lunch bags into a kitchen-sized trash bag.

Drop off at your local homeless shelter or hand out in an area where you have noticed many homeless. For shelters, call ahead first to check on drop off times.

3. Make No-Sew Fleece Blankets

No-sew fleece blankets are used by many different charities to comfort babies, foster children, children in the hospital, the homeless, pets, and more. To make a Lightweight Blanket, you'll need a yard and a half of fleece for child-size or two yards for adult size (can tie two pieces together for a heavier blanket), scissors or rotary cutter and mat, and a tape measure. Go to pebbletossers.org for detailed instructions. Trim off edges. Then, cut out squares off each corner, so the blanket looks like a large plus sign. With the remaining edges, cut 4" by 1" fringe (1" wide and 4" deep). Tie the two fringe pieces next to each other together or knot each individual fringe. Fold it, and then roll it up and tie it with string.

Drop off at your local homeless shelter, favorite charity that supports the troops, animal shelter, fire or police station, or refugee organization. These are needed in the winter!

4. Make Happy Cards

Cards should be cheery, with sentiments of Have a Great Day, Thinking about You, You're Special, Happy Birthday, and so on. If you want to make birthday cards, please keep those in a separate bag. Construction paper, stationery, craft paper, or printer paper are typically used and cut in half for a finished size card of around 4 by 5 inches. Get creative with stickers, glitter, or magazine cut-outs.

Drop off to a local veteran's organization, refugee organization, fire or police station, or children's hospital. Hand out yourself (or with your kids) at a senior citizen center. Make sure to call first to see if they will accept cards (some children's hospitals do not). Add some cookies if you're dropping a letter of gratitude off to your local police or fire station.

5. Give out Toiletry/Hygiene Kits

Hygiene kits contain items that many of us take for granted, such as a toothbrush or soap. However, many foster children or homeless people do not have daily access to such items. Since these items are used daily, there is always a need for more. Visit The Packaged Good, where they have all the supplies for you ready to go during drop-in periods (thepackagedgood.org) or host a party for your friends or coworkers to pack care packages together. You can also do this at home. Decorate a card with a positive message and add in soap, toothpaste, toothbrush, and shampoo in a re-sealable plastic bag.

Drop off to the local homeless shelter, refugee organization, community center, or school; leave some in your car and hand out when you see someone in need.

6.   Make Happy Paper Chains

Cut out strips of paper 2" by 6" or whatever size you prefer and write happy things on them, then link together into a chain. Staple the end together to secure each link. Make the chain as long as you need.

Drop off to senior center, children's hospital, or refugee organization. Call first to make sure they can use it.

7.   Paint Flowerpots (and Other Crafts) for Seniors

A painted flowerpot with bright colors and creative images can brighten anyone's room. Fill the pot with a small flower, like a marigold or a zinnia, and you've got a complete gift. This project can be done alongside a senior resident at an assisted living or off-site and delivered. Use sharpies or permanent paint to draw designs, images, quotes, and so on. The pots can be sprayed with polyurethane for permanence. Tip: Be sure to line the bottom of the pot with a coffee filter (cut to size) to catch any dirt from falling out the bottom. It's best to use potting soil that is suited for containers and has fertilizer and water retention materials premixed with the soil. Place the pot on a small plastic lid or plate to catch any excess water.

Other ideas include a painted picture frame, a decorated cup with a notepad and pens inside, a child's artwork to decorate their walls, or care packages with toiletry items such as shampoo, lotion, and soap.

Donate to an assisted living facility near you. They can be placed in their residents' rooms, in the gathering rooms, on dining room tables, and so on. But the best gift is your visit. Deliver it yourself.

8.   Various Drives

Set up a donation drive at your school, church, or temple; in your neighborhood; or with a club or group. The following items can be collected for donations:

- **Used towels and blankets:** Donate to any pet rescue group.
- **Gently Used iPods and MP3 players:** Donate to any assisted living center. Be sure to reset the device before donating it. Age-appropriate music is uploaded to the device, and then the senior citizens are taught how to use them. Excellent for Alzheimer's patients.
- **Gently Used Shoes:** Keep old shoes out of landfills and give them a new life. Research a local organization that refurbishes shoes or nonprofit thrift store.
- **Toiletries:** Travel sized items are always needed to assemble hygiene kits. Most needed items: toothbrushes, toothpaste, deodorant, soap, nail files, hand lotion, socks, combs, hand sanitizer. Drop off at The Packaged Good or local homeless shelter.
- **Nonperishable Food:** Canned items such as vegetables, fruits, meats, boxes of pasta, cereal, snack items, Ramen noodles, peanut butter, jelly, and cake mixes are always needed at local food pantries. Donate to local food pantries.
- **Party in a Bag:** People who obtain their food from food pantries love the opportunity to get a party in a bag. Assemble any of the following in a decorative gift bag: cake mix, tub of frosting, packet of candles, streamers, colorful plates and napkins, disposable cake pan, balloons, small party favors. Donate to local food pantries.

Reach out to local animal shelters, homeless shelters, and food pantries to see what's on their hot list to collect. They always have a handful of items that are needed most.

9. Entertainment for Seniors or Rehabilitation Centers

Have a special talent? Use it for good. Teach a dance or art class at an assisted living facility. Perform a dance or sing a song. Simply give your time and play bingo. It will make their day. Can you teach a computer class or help people learn about budgeting? Rehabilitation centers are always looking for talent to help their clients get self-sufficient.

Contact a local assisted living facility or rehabilitation center and ask for the activity director.

10. Set up a Lemonade Stand or Bake Sale

Bake some cookies and make some lemonade. Set up a table and chairs and make a sign that says which charity the money will be donated to. $1 per item is reasonable.

Donate the money to your favorite charity. They all need monetary support.

11. Pick up Trash at a Nearby Park

Some parks have organized trash pickup day, but no need to wait for them. Go now and pick up all the trash you see. Make it fun by bringing along friends; see who can find the most random items or pick up the most trash.

These last four projects are a little more in-depth, for older kids or adults:

12. Host a Party

Host an event for underprivileged kids in your area. Partner with local homeless shelters or schools. Bring in pizza, jumpy houses, and snow cones for a fun day. If you're in Atlanta, reach out to Creating Connected Communities or Children Helping Children to help host events for kids in need.

13. Raise Money for Your Favorite Charity

Organize a race or party to raise money for your favorite charity. If you're in Atlanta, check out Kids Boost. They can help guide you on how to use your talents to raise money in a big way for charity. Three siblings who lost their father raised over $20,000 for Kate's Club, an organization that helps families who have lost a loved one. They hosted a race to raise the money. Kristen at Kid's Boost can guide your child through the process. Must be over age eight.

14. Use a Talent to Help a Local Nonprofit

Create marketing videos, write marketing copy, teach an accounting or computer class. If you're in Atlanta, Pebble Tossers can help you channel your talents for good.

15. Grow a Garden for Good

Create your own garden in your yard and bring your vegetables to the local food pantry or food bank. There are also neighborhoods groups and organizations that have community gardens that you can reach out to for harvesting fruits and vegetables for good.

Want to create a customized volunteer plan for your teen? Reach out to Pebble Tossers to set it up. Pebble Tossers' website has a robust list of weekly family volunteer opportunities available for many of our favorite charities below.

Sally and Jen's Favorite Charities

The Packaged Good   **www.thepackagedgood.org**

On a mission to instill in children the desire to give back while inspiring the next generation of giving, The Packaged Good provides a fun, inspirational environment where kids and community groups can decorate and personalize care packages and create craft projects for people in need. Whether it's giving to our armed forces, the elderly, the homeless, or hospitalized kids, The Packaged Good partners with vetted, reputable, nonprofit organizations to allow volunteers the ability to support causes closest to their hearts while handling all the logistics.

Pebble Tossers   **www.pebbletossers.org**

Pebble Tossers is a youth service organization and family volunteering resource that makes it easy to find fun, age-appropriate service projects for kids and teens in metro Atlanta. Pebble Tossers has a great newsletter and website that lists all the events in Atlanta where you and your kids can do good. They also will track volunteer hours for your teen as well as set up a customized volunteer plan.

Creating Connected Communities   **www.cccprojects.org**

Creating Connected Communities was formed with the mission of providing Atlanta teens with tools and resources to assist people in need and to teach them fundraising, public speaking, and project management skills. The goal is that these teen volunteers will learn about community outreach and leadership while organizing and planning Amy's Holiday Party, which brings holiday cheer to hundreds of homeless, refugee, and orphaned children. Teen volunteers run and manage events and parties for underprivileged youth throughout the year.

Community Assistance Center   **www.ourcac.org**

Community Assistance Center (CAC) was founded in 1987 to centralize assistance to those in need. CAC has grown and is now supported by congregations of all faiths, businesses, schools, civic groups, and individuals. CAC is a City of Sandy Springs agency, a Fulton County Human Services agency, and a United Way agency. They provide compassionate assistance to neighbors in need by providing financial support, helping to meet basic needs and promoting self-reliance. You can volunteer in their thrift shop or food pantry, or at one of their events. Most volunteer opportunities are for teens and adults, but small children can help stock the food pantry.

Rainbow Village   **www.rainbowvillage.org**

Rainbow Village is a community of transformation for homeless families with children from across Georgia. Most of the heads-of-households are women who have fled lives full of domestic violence and poverty. These families find refuge, recover, and learn to rebuild their lives with the love and support of a safe haven surrounding them. Rainbow Village's program offers a long-term solution through support services for the entire family. Volunteer opportunities include making and serving dinner, helping with the grounds, and providing tutoring and talent services. Most volunteer opportunities are for teens and adults. Families can serve dinners.

Mary Hall Freedom House   **www.maryhallfreedomhouse.org**

Mary Hall Freedom House is a nonprofit organization and national leader in gender-specific treatment, recovery, housing, and support services to help women and women with children break the cycle of poverty, homelessness, mental health disorders, and addiction. Mary Hall Freedom House's current capacity can provide housing and services to over two hundred single women and over 75 children on any given day, restoring over five hundred lives annually, and has served more than five thousand women since 1996. Volunteer opportunities include making and serving dinner, taking care of the children, and providing tutoring and talent services. Most volunteer opportunities are for teens and adults. Families can serve dinners.

Children's Healthcare of Atlanta   www.choa.org

At Children's Healthcare of Atlanta, the doctors, nurses, and staff are specially trained to care for children under the age of twenty-one. From colorful, friendly waiting rooms to equipment that fits patients of all sizes, every detail is designed specifically for kids. They provide world-class care in more than sixty pediatric specialties, and all the specialist understand that children's medical and emotional needs are different from adults. Volunteer opportunities include helping with events and interacting with the kids with games and crafts. Most opportunities are for teens and adults.

New American Pathways   www.newamericanpathways.org

New American Pathways provides approximately four thousand refugees per year with the necessary tools to rebuild their lives and achieve long-term success. New American Pathways' vision is to promote safety, stability, success, and service for individual refugees and refugee families in Georgia. Most opportunities are for teens and adults.

Malachi's Storehouse   www.malachisstorehouse.org

Malachi's Storehouse is dedicated to addressing food insecurity in metro Atlanta. They are an outreach ministry of St. Patrick's Episcopal Church, providing both groceries and a hot meal for those in need of emergency support.

Operation Stars and Stripes   operationstarsandstripes.org

Operation Stars & Stripes is an all-volunteer 501 (c) (3) not-for-profit organization dedicated to supporting America's military with requested care packages and letters. Volunteer opportunities for adults include helping pack care packages. Children can write letters.

Hugs for Soldiers   www.hugsforsoldiers.org

Founded in 2003, Hugs for Soldiers is dedicated to offering comforts from home and brightening a Soldier's day with a care package, card, or letter of encouragement. Their adopted troops, who are deployed thousands of miles away from home, need to be reassured that America cares about them. They provide love and support for our nation's military who make daily sacrifices for the freedom America enjoys. Volunteer opportunities for adults include helping pack care packages. Children can write letters.

Veteran's Empowerment Organization   www.veohero.org

Established in 2008, VEO's mission is to provide housing, supportive services, job training, and placement to veterans on their journey to an empowered life. Since its founding, VEO has served more than two thousand homeless veterans. VEO is working to create a more humane world where poverty is alleviated for veterans, our communities are supportive of the needs of veterans, and all veterans can develop their full potential.

Jewish Families & Career Services   www.jfcs-atlanta.org

JF&CS helps improve the quality of life and build self-sufficiency in individuals and families in greater Atlanta. Their goal is to build a community of empowered lives by making hope and opportunity happen.

They provide counselling and career services for older adults and individuals with intellectual and developmental disabilities and free dental care through the Ben Massell Clinic.

Kids Boost   www.kidsboost.org

This is an Atlanta area nonprofit that inspires and equips kids eight to eighteen to give back to their communities and world. They provide coaching to guide children on how to use their passion and talents to raise money for their favorite charity.

Ronald McDonald House   www.armhc.org

The mission of Atlanta Ronald McDonald House Charities is to nurture the health and well-being of children and families. Over the past thirty-seven years, over forty-six thousand families have called them home. With two locations in Atlanta, Ronald McDonald House Charities has eighty bedrooms and features a separate wing for transplant patients. More than five hundred meals are prepared by the Atlanta community to support the families during their stay. Volunteer opportunities include making and serving meals and interacting with the families through crafts and games.

Homeless at Heart   www.homelessatheart.org

An eleven-year-old Atlanta student's aspiration to make Valentine boxes in January 2015 resulted in Homeless at Heart giving away more than thirteen thousand boxes, bags, and handwritten Valentine cards in 2017 in Atlanta, Birmingham, Oklahoma City, and Albany, Georgia. They now host Valentine box packing and partner with Pebble Tossers and The Packaged Good on MLK Day for a large packing event for the homeless.

A.G. Rhodes Health & Rehab   www.agrhodes.org

A.G. Rhodes provides expert and compassionate rehabilitation therapy and residential care to seniors in metro Atlanta. As a not-for-profit organization, they can provide the highest standard of care, which includes post-surgical recovery, therapeutic rehabilitation, and skilled nursing. Volunteer opportunities include visiting the residents and playing games, providing a talent, or helping with an event.

Creating Your Volunteer Plan

By Jennifer Guynn, Founder and Executive Director of Pebble Tossers

It is very easy to go about our days with our heads down. But after reading this book, you are probably thinking to yourself that it may be time to raise your head and do something special and meaningful.

Sally found a way to honor Grover through founding The Packaged Good and a way to leave a legacy in his honor. She and her daughters were also able to heal through giving. Whether you want to leave a legacy or are just inspired to do something to help others or to make your life more fulfilled, this section provides suggestions for little everyday changes that can end up making a big difference in your community.

Here are three helpful steps to guide your volunteer journey:

Step 1: Start Small. My husband tells me the only way to eat an elephant is one bite at a time. The same goes for starting any new adventure. Trying to decide what you want to do with your life takes some serious thought. How do you figure out how to care and what matters to you? Give yourself the luxury of time. Set aside time to wonder, to imagine, and to brainstorm. Keep a journal nearby for brilliant nuggets that pop into your head. Sally took time off from work to foster her creative energy and for her idea to arrive.

Start by thinking of three things that make you happy and three that make you mad. Something like "I love when historic buildings are preserved" or "Seeing cigarette butts on the ground makes me mad." Those six things will set the course toward what you want to help or change. You can then narrow it down to one or two items. Maybe they are related; it's up to you.

Step 2: Think Big (and Visualize). You may think this contradicts Step 1. Well, if you have started small, you have no place to go but up. Take the thing that ticks you off the most. What would happen if that thing were no longer an issue? For example, if childhood hunger infuriates you, how would you see the world differently if that problem were solved? What would have to happen to make that go away? What could you do to help one child not go to bed hungry for one night? One week? One month?

Keep asking yourself questions. Then ask more questions. Research the questions. Become one with Google. Asking questions led us to the development of electricity and the discovery of penicillin; keep asking questions. Through your questions, eventually you will seek others who know more about a subject than you do. They will have some answers, but just as importantly, they will share your passion for the subject. From there, dialogue begins, plans are made, and action is taken. Thinking big can happen fast, or it can take a lifetime. That all depends on how well you did when you started small.

Step 3: Believe in Yourself. Believing that you can do something can take you to great lengths. Then find someone else who believes in you too.

When my kids were little, we would read to them each night. One book would always lead to two. When my son was about three years old, he began "reading". He actually could not read, but he believed he could. He would listen to his older sisters read, and he just knew he could do it too. He would pick the same book and would turn the pages and "read" the story. He had memorized the pages and perfected the inflection in his voice, pausing when appropriate, and it certainly looked and sounded like he could read. That belief that he could read gave him the confidence to try other books, and he then became eager to try new things.

Sally believed in herself and in The Packaged Good concept, and she was able to overcome any challenges that came her way because her belief in the idea and her confidence were so strong.

Once you go through these three simple steps, you will begin to formulate your own volunteer plan. You may have ideas for what you want to do but not know where to go. If you are in Atlanta, you can meet with Pebble Tossers, The Packaged Good, or one of our favorite charities we listed in the book.

A few years ago, I read about two young sisters, ages five and three, who collected their dollar-a-week allowance for five weeks and donated the $5 to PAWS Animal Shelter. Was that $5 significant to the operations of PAWS? No. But was it significant to the staff and the board and the other volunteers? Absolutely. That small donation was a big deal to those sisters, who gave up something in order to make it. I am so proud of their parents, too, for not discouraging their donation because it was small. Those girls received the same good benefit as someone who donated $500, and it inspired them to do more.

In 2010, I received an envelope in the mail from two elementary school girls who collected $14.22 at their lemonade stand because they heard about Pebble Tossers and wanted to help. I saved their handwritten note; it means the world to me. These girls did something with a purpose and on purpose. I wrote them a thank-you note and hand-delivered it.

I want to highlight some amazing stories about how making a small change can have a huge impact on the community.

Tim and Becky O'Mara: Bearings Bike Shop. They saw a problem. They unknowingly started a solution. They cared and became significant to someone else.

Tim and Becky believe firmly in the value of exchange: Everyone has something to offer regardless of their socio-economic status. Adair Park residents were frustrated by the litter and dumping that tormented their streets. Neighbors saw value in helping keep the neighborhood clean. The idea was born: Kids would be invited to earn a bike by picking up trash in the neighborhood. With that, everyone won; neighbors were thrilled the community was being cleaned up, and kids were thrilled to get a new bike.

In the process, a model was established: Give a kid a bike, and he will simply ride it wherever he goes, but let him earn the bike, and you can make him a part of the community. Make him a contributing member of his family and community, and you have the makings of a confident, responsible, and healthy child who has a significantly less chance of falling into a life of crime and violence, and a child who sees the support of a community that values his contribution.

Bearings Bike Shop now has three locations along the Atlanta BeltLine; participating kids have earned 575 bikes, made 6,500 bike repairs and have logged over forty-three hundred hours learning about repairs. Learn more about Bearings Bike shop online: www.bearingsbikeshop.org

Aaliyah Rucker: A Touch of Warmth. When Aaliyah Rucker was four years old, she loved blankets. She had one in every room and took one with her everywhere. That Thanksgiving, they were cleaning out closets, and she didn't want to give away a favorite one. Her mom explained that some kids didn't have blankets of their own, and that upset Aaliyah. She asked friends and neighbors for used blankets and donated them to a shelter. This idea of sharing blankets stayed with Aaliyah and led her to start her own foundation, A Touch of Warmth Foundation. Aaliyah is now fourteen years old and has given away over twelve thousand blankets to the homeless, seniors citizens, children's hospitals, and soldiers. She organizes collection drives and hosts bake sales and other fundraisers so she can purchase new blankets or buy fleece to make blankets. She talks to groups of students and inspires others to care. She talks to groups of adults and inspires them to do more. She and her mom took something that was small yet meaningful to them and thought big. Learn more about A Touch of Warmth online: www.atouchofwarmth.org

ALS Ice Bucket Challenge. When Pete Frates issued the first Ice Bucket Challenge, he was doing so to increase awareness of the disease and to increase funding toward finding a cure for ALS. The movement went viral after that, touching most of the country, from fourth grade social studies classes to Little League coaches to celebrities to public officials. It raised over $85 million in 2014 and has raised hundreds of millions of dollars since.

The ALS Ice Bucket Challenge is a way to level the philanthropic playing field for kids. They want to make a difference, and this provided a fun and edgy way to participate in a socially conscience way. Here's why I think this challenge helps kids become social active:

1. It's easy to do. The beauty of this challenge is that anyone with access to water can complete the task. There doesn't need to be much thought to the process. Too often, adults overcomplicate a volunteer experience for kids. But with this action, anyone can grab a container of water, add ice, grab a phone to record, dump ice water, and you're done. You just completed a philanthropic act.

2. It's empowering. The concept is that anyone can accept the challenge. Anyone. Even if you are not able to send in a donation, you are still raising awareness of the disease. More kids are now aware that there is no cure to ALS, that it is a fatal disease. They now feel connected to the greater effort of finding a cure by participating.

3. It's a sacrifice. It's often said that to help someone else, you have to give something of your own, usually in the form of time, talent, or treasure. Agreeing to being showered with ice water, however crazy it seems, is a sacrifice. Kids take this tangible effort, experience the frigid water with all five senses, and know they have done something good. It will make a lasting impression that they were a part of something bigger than themselves; they will always remember their first ALS Ice Bucket Challenge.

4. It leads to the next step. Many kids have been introduced to ALS through the challenge. They have seen their friends' Instagram posts and watched others complete challenges and noticed that not everyone does it to promote ALS; some choose to promote another charity. This is a great opportunity for families to open discussions about issues they find important. From these discussions, families can find ways to help an organization tied to that issue. Do you have an animal lover in the family? Begin a drive to collect old towels or blankets to donate to the local Humane Society. Do you know someone with cancer? September is National Childhood Cancer Awareness Month, and many organizations have walks or events to raise funds for research; sign up and participate.

Kids are trying to figure out where they fit in this world and know they want to make a positive difference. We can smile and move on to the next item on our busy list, or we can encourage them and guide them through the process of learning how to be socially active participants in making that positive difference. Pouring icy water over their heads can be how they start their own ripple of giving.

For help discovering your own volunteer plan, please contact pebbletossers.org.

Appendix

A Collection of Poems by Grover Mundell

Pineapple Dream

Yesterday
in a pineapple dream,
there were red
and yellow
blue
and green,
and everywhere it seemed

a turtle
looked into my eyes.
Why are you here?
Where are you from?
An ancient being in disguise,
we let him be
and got out of the sea.

Ukulele music
danced on the air;
smiling and happy
I shook out my hair.
Some call it paradise.
We were there

We were there
in a pineapple dream
with spinner dolphins jumping
out the clear blue sea.

Do you remember
yesterday
with me?

Gemini

There are two babies in here,
and sure enough there they were
on the ultrasound monitor.
You're kidding!
No, I'm not

Wow ...
Twins.
And I just heard from Jim,
who got married a couple
months after I did
after years of bachelorhood,
after devastating divorces,
after similar simmering
misogynistic
tendencies.
We had both gotten
married again,
and then just yesterday
he sent a message
they were having twins.

I remember telling him
that I was getting married
and how he had replied,
Me too!
And now this,
a minor miracle.

How were we going to do it?
One seemed like an adventure,
but two?!
At once ...

My wife looked at me
and started laughing.
Apparently the blood
had drained from my face,
and my expression
gave away my fears.

But inside
my heart was racing.
It was really going to happen:
I was going to be a father.
What a moment.

I watched
as she kept struggling
with the ultrasound wand
as a million thoughts raced
through my head.
I watched as the strip monitor
streamed across the screen.

I'm sorry,
but I'm not getting a heartbeat
on either one
of the babies.
I'm really sorry ...

Chores

I'm going down to milk the Guernsey cow.
I'll be back with milk and cream.
If you'd like to come, I'll show you how
to feel the rhythm of the stream.

We'll brave the crispness in the morning air,
dawn breaking scooping Guernsey's grain.
Lovingly patting, brushing her hair,
bringing her up the familiar lane.

The tone at first is tin and hollow,
streaming down to shiny pale,
and filling rounder sounds will follow
with even tempo of her swishing tail.

Old Guernsey gives me more than milk and cream;
she keeps my world upon its track.
It's all in the rhythm with the stream,
and tomorrow morning I'll be back.

Ode to a Mockingbird

He was singing sweetly
on a summer night so late:
a mockingbird busily building a nest
unwittingly—his fate.

The entire farm could hear him sing
his soothing lullaby,
nesting near up in the roof
above me where I lie.

I was ten and foolish then.
I owned a pellet gun,
so after several sleepless nights,
I swore this bird was done.

I stalked him in the garden;
I felled him from a tree,
though as I ran and picked him up,
I did so mournfully.

He seemed to ask a question,
a simple question why,
What have I done to anyone
that I should have to die?

I didn't have an answer then,
and still just questions now.
Why would I silence any song?
I can't imagine how.

I still can't sleep with restful bliss,
no birdsong in my ears.
More frightening is the silence
with me lo so many years.

I've prayed a mockingbird would
come
and nest in nearby tree
so I could slumber in his song,
his soothing melody.

Checkered Past

A little boy
and his Granddad playing checkers—
Grandad played to win,
and win often he did.

To create competition,
he would set his board
with checkers two less
so that I could win when I played my best.

Time went on,
and one less checker.
Time went on;
my game got better
till that last game
played even up.

In those days,
Grandad would read poetry—
tales of McGrew Dangerous Dan,
the magical Touch of the Master's Hand,
and Casey's hit heard 'round the land.

Now I write for him a poem
and visit him in the old folks' home,
and I'll give up a checker or even two
if that's what it takes to play with you.
Perhaps we can read a poem or two.

Phantom Cat

He came up the stairs
and looked in the door.
I never heard him,
but suddenly
there he was.

Sleek
like a silent killer in the night—
like a panther.

Someone else's
house cat.

I tried to coax him in,
but
he slipped away.

He didn't trust me,
didn't want to take a chance
with the likes of what he saw.

Why do they come around,
why do they turn away,
and why
do I want them
to
want
me?

Suky Luky Bongo

Growing up
around my house,
we all knew
when Tater was
happy.

He would sing.

Nothing recognizable
even as "music"
but it would go on
like humpback whale song.

Bending to his work,
his hammer
banging exclamation points
into this exotic improv.

Life became chant—
a symphony
of clanging tools,
primitive vocalizations,
and pounding
of "ole stub."

With cooperative fate,
this could go late—
for hours
into demented night.

He's open that way,
doesn't mind others
bearing witness
to his joy

or
his anger.

When chant abruptly ended,
interrupted
and formed words again, emerged
as curses
loud and angry.

Aimed at conspiring gods,
hurling tests at his toil
by way of unyielding metal

that which
would soon melt
beneath
his fiery torch
or bend and break
beneath his sledge.

Growing up
around my house,
we all knew
when Tater was
unhappy.

Night Time

Monsters and strangers
outside the door,
but Daddy is here
inside.

Tickles and giggles
even the score
and brush all fear
aside.

A nursery rhyme,
a song sung by two,
a lullaby
whispered low.

The moon peeks in
with a tender grin,
and off to sleep we go.

Rhapsody

Hear the angels up above—
I'm in Love!
A life fulfilling fantasy, it's you I'm dreaming of.
My heart screams, screams, screams
To enchant and to delight.
Be my blessed everything,
be my brilliant brassy ring
in the shadows of the night.
Feel the beat, beat, beat
of my heart beneath the sheet
from the cadence of the cosmos and from somewhere up above.
I'm in love, I'm in love,
I'm in love, I'm in love.
Through the screaming and beating, I'm in love.

You're Not a Superhero

A big pillow
slid off the bed
onto the lamp cord.

I sprang across the room,
catching it (the lamp) in midair.

That really was close,
Ruby exclaimed
several times
in succession.

Thanks to my
cat-like quickness
and reflexes,
I've saved the day,

I joked.

You're not a superhero;
you're just a daddy.
Superheroes don't save lamps,
they save the planet.

You're not a superhero;
just a daddy.
Are you trying to be
the best daddy you can be?

That's what God wants to know.

Always

I am always, always with you.
Don't you forget it.
Not a single moment
do I regret together.

You are always, always with me
here in my heart,
precious family
we started together.

They bring me to tears—
it's overwhelming.

I love our home,
though there may be rats
occasionally.

It's our own,
and it's love that's shining down.
Look out and see.

I am always, always with you.
Don't you forget it.
Not a single moment
do I regret together.

You are always, always with me
here in my heart,
precious family
we started together.

They bring me to tears.
You bring me to tears.

Nurse Yvonne

They come creeping
into my room
at 1
at 2
at 3 and at 4

wanting pee
and blood
and air
and more.

In blue
and white
every night—
every morning too.

Those beautiful
angels of mercy,
they come for me,
they come
for you.

Gentle as the daffodil,
effortless
through the clay,
soon arrives the day

I'll be on my way
while others
stay

Here
Near
Angels
on cat feet

And pray.

Make It on to Emory

Just make it
through the night—
everything's
going to be all right.

Make it on to Emory.

They are toasting
out in Philly,
in the isles
of San Juan.

I grasp the waves
of power—
just keep
keeping on.

Up from Texas
too many to name
from places all over,
nexus the same.

But on the homeland plains
of Baca—
damn right they raising

Hell.

I feel hearts
as big as life itself
Praying.

Wish me well.

I started slipping under.
Sally …
knows always what to do,
rounded up the doctors,
took me back to ICU.

Don't let that number fall
boy,
you got too much
riding on you.

Matilda and Ruby
They need to make it
to
Emory
too.

On the Mend

A walk in the park
every night at eight,
trying to rehab—
the hip's been replaced.

Harkens back years:
boyhood chores,
milking the cow
each early morn.

Though I dreaded the chore,
I thrived on my time
once I got down to the barn.

It's now the same.
Click, click, click.

My cane on the pavement,
my soul on the mend,
I have to wear my weakness
at the end of my sleeve.

And the dogs bark
along the winding trail,
and people all greet
the clicking cane.

I struggle.

My arm numbing
and my legs becoming
rubbery
as click, click, clicking
merges
with sounds of milk
ringing
down to a metal bucket.

My calves burn,
and I feel good about it all
for the first time
in quite a while.

References

1. Gladwell, Malcom. *David and Goliath.* 2013.
2. Yörük, Baris. *Journal of Economic Psychology*, 45, December 2014, pp. 71–83. "Does giving to charity lead to better health?"
3. Norton, Michael, Elizabeth Dunn, Lara Aknin. *Science,* 2008. "Spending Money on Others Promotes Happiness."
4. UC Berkeley Study on Volunteerism and Health, 1999.
5. Moll, Jorge, Jordan Grafman. *Proceedings of the National Academy of Sciences of the United States of America.* "Human fronto-mesolimbic networks guide decisions about charitable donation."
6. *JAMA Pediatrics.* April 2013.
7. Ranapurwala, Shabbar. *Springer Open.* "Volunteering in adolescence and young adulthood crime involvement: a longitudinal analysis from the add health study."
8. Brown, Brene. Daring Greatly: *How the Courage to Be Vulnerable Transforms the Way We Live, Love, Parent, and Lead,* 2012.
9. Phelan, Thomas. *1,2, 3 Magic.* 2003.

Message of Gratitude

I am so grateful for my village:
My loves Ruby and Matilda, for being supportive of this book,
my family (the Goldbergs and the Mundells) for being supportive of
sharing my story and providing my foundation.

Jen Guynn of Pebble Tossers for partnering with me to do good, co-writing
the giving guide, and writing the volunteer guide.

A special thanks to the people who helped me make this book happen:
Maggie Klein, Brian Mand, Louis Goldberg, Jenn Riehn, Heather Wilson,
Angie Goldberg, and Beth Walkup. Thank you to Beth for the beautiful
cover design.

My mentors for believing in me, guiding me, and inspiring me:
Sara Blakely, Louis Goldberg, Brian Hankin, Greg Foglesong, and Laurie
Ann Goldman.

My girlfriends for supporting me (some even editing the book!):
Lori, Angie, Kristi, Paige, Jenn, Elisa, Dale, Julie, Maggie, Liz, Lydia,
Ilana, Lesli, Laura, Eti, Tracy, Vanda, Lori, Liz, Heather, Elizabeth.

The Packaged Good Dream Team:
Laura, Lesli, Lydia, Ilana, Sam, Lisa and Joanna

Temple Emanu-El and Rabbi Spike and Marita Anderson for the support.

To my Spanx family, thank you for the love and support.

And thank you to my new family Kids II!

I also want to highlight The Packaged Good supporters, friends, and advisors who helped me make a difference and get The Packaged Good up and running.

Founding Families

Sara Blakely Foundation
Elizabeth Davis and Family
Fried, Rogers & Goldberg, LLP
The Goldberg Family/Pediatric Health Center of Dunwoody
The Lazarian Family
Billi Marcus Foundation
The Mundell Family
Regency Centers
The Schilling Family/Financial Innovations

Friends and Advisors

Amy Agami
All Around Construction
Lydia Anderson
Jennifer Babbit Bodner
Carolyn and Joey Bauman
Camp Barney Medintz
Elisa and Sloan Crumbley
Andrew Etkind
Josh Feingold
Harrison Frank
Laurie Ann Goldman
Lesli Greenberg
Jesse Grossman
Barb Hamilton
Brian Hankin
Amy Helman-Darley
Tracy and Mitch Hires
Sonny and Julie Hires

Maggie Klein
Jason Miller
Jon Miller
Justin Milrad
Joey Reiman
Amy and Philip Rubin
Dawn Sams
Rob and Allie Shields/Acadia Shutters and Blinds
Mark Silberman
Jason Smith
Liz Stanton
Melanie and Tony Sussman
Ilana Tolk
Dawn and Eric Tresh
Steve Peltier and Diana Tsiang
Itai Tsur

In-Kind Partners

GoGo SqueeZ
Henry Schein and Colgate
Jeckil Promotions
Office Creations
PaperCraft

Grants and Family Foundations

Atlanta Senior Care Networking Niche
Bennett Thrasher Foundation
Coldwell Banker Cares
Douglas J. Hertz Family Foundation, Inc.
Sidney & Lillian Klemow Foundation, Inc.

CPSIA information can be obtained
at www.ICGtesting.com
Printed in the USA
LVOW03*0531171117
556450LV00002B/2/P